ALSO AVAILABLE FROM HANS BEUMER

AUDIT RISK MANAGEMENT

DRIVING AUDIT VALUE (VOL. II)

The best practice strategy guide for minimising the audit risks and achieving the internal audit strategies and objectives

HANS BEUMER

HB Publications
Zug, Switzerland
www.hansbeumer.com

First edition published in March 2017

This book is available as:
-Hardcover: ISBN 978-3-906861-15-9
-EBook: ISBN 978-3-906861-16-6

Printed and distributed by Lulu Press, Inc

CONTENTS

FOREWORD

Many thousands of pages in many hundreds of books have been written about risk-based internal auditing, enterprise risk management, internal audit's focus on identifying and mitigating the company's risks to achieving its business strategies and objectives, the role of the audit function in supporting management and the board with risk mitigation, and so forth.

To the contrary, there is no literature on the topic of managing the risks of the internal audit function itself. This is uncharted territory. That is very surprising, because the audit function should be managed like a business by the Chief Audit Executive (CAE). As any other (part of) business, the audit function is just as exposed to the risk of not-achieving its objectives. The audit function's risks to the achievement of the audit strategies and objectives, and the prevention and mitigation of these audit risks, are the topics of this book.

Audit Risk Management differs from all the other books about internal audit, in the way it combines the theoretical knowledge with the practical experiences of a seasoned CAE:

- This is the first and only book that develops a clear audit risk identification, measurement and mitigation strategy for the internal audit function. It reflects on the audit function from an entirely new perspective by defining the risks of not-achieving the audit strategies and objectives, by analysing the audit risk drivers and the audit risks, and by presenting the solutions for the mitigation of those risks.

- The *Beumer Audit Risk Management Model©* provides transparency for the risk management of the audit function. The model creates a unique new frame of reference for managing the risks to the audit customer value proposition.

- This book includes the practical experiences, examples, tips and foremost solutions, from an experienced CAE. The content of this book draws upon 28 years of business experience, of which 16 years as leader of audit functions of globally operating corporations.

Audit Risk Management is the best practice guide for ensuring internal audit's success in the company. Follow the strategic risk management principles explained in this book to becoming successful in achieving the objectives of the audit function. Apply the fundamental audit risk management principles and a successful career as CAE is easily attainable.

This book is part of a series on internal audit best practices called *Driving Audit Value*. The first three books in the series are:

1. *Audit Function Strategy*: This *Volume I* of *Driving Audit Value* describes the strategies for creating the maximum audit added value at the level of the internal audit function. The book explains and analyses the two main value drivers and the six main value enablers. *Volume I* was published in January 2017 (see the book preview and the global endorsements on pages 201 to 204).

2. *Audit Risk Management*: The *Beumer Audit Risk Management Model*© provides a ground-breaking new approach to understanding, identifying, measuring and mitigating the audit risks at both the audit function level and the audit engagement level. This book focuses solely on identifying and mitigating 60 potential audit risks. These audit risk management measures are described in *Driving Audit Value, Volume II*.

3. *Audit Engagement Strategy*: The strategic model for driving the audit value at the level of the audit engagements is described in *Driving Audit Value, Volume III*, which will be available from July 2017. At the audit engagement level, the audit added value, value drivers, and value enablers also exist, though with a different content when compared to the level of the audit function (see the book preview on pages 205 and 206).

Books published under "The Successful Business Series" describe the professional experiences in various lines of business. The Series has the intention of helping you make your business successful.

Read to advance your life,
drs. Hans Beumer
March 2017

BOOK STRUCTURE

This book provides a practical approach and concrete tools to manage the audit risks at both the audit function and the audit engagement levels. The model for managing the risks of not-achieving the audit (function and engagement) objectives is reflected in the four parts of the book:

PART I: Audit Risk Management
Part I presents the *Beumer Audit Risk Management Model*©. This model shows the comprehensive audit risk management framework for driving the audit risk identification, measurement and mitigation. The model connects 60 audit risks, in 6 audit risk categories, to 30 audit objectives. Depending on the risk appetite and the audit risk prevention, the CAE can choose from 66 audit risk mitigation measures for reducing the audit risks to an acceptable level. The *Audit Assurance Risk Management Model*© and the *Audit Process Risk Management Model*© show the relationships between the objectives, the risks and the risk mitigation, as the individual building blocks of the strategy model. Part I explains that the risk appetite is the most important driver for the level of the risk as well as the risk mitigation. The *Audit Function Risk Indicators Model*© enables the CAE to quickly grasp the risk profile of the audit function.

PART II: Audit Objectives
Part II describes the 6 main audit objective categories for value, focus, execution, performance, reporting, and compliance. The *Audit Objectives Catalogue*© captures the 30 audit objectives in the structure of the 6 audit objective categories, split into the audit assurance objectives and the audit process objectives.

PART III: Audit Risks
Part III defines the audit risk and explains the nature and details of the 60 individual audit risks, captured in the 6 main audit risk categories: value risk, focus risk, execution risk, performance risk, reporting risk, and compliance risk. The *Audit Assurance Risk Tree*© shows the 33 audit assurance related risks, whereas the *Audit Process Risk Tree*© shows the 27 audit process related risks. For each of the 6

audit risk categories, a risk matrix matches the audit risks from the *Audit Risks Catalogue*© to the audit objectives from the *Audit Objectives Catalogue*©. Additionally, a risk map matches the audit risks from the *Audit Risks Catalogue*© to the audit function's customer value proposition.

PART IV: Audit Risk Mitigation

Part IV presents the *Audit Risk Mitigation Catalogue*©, listing 66 risk mitigation measures, divided into the *Audit Assurance Risk Mitigation Tree*© (36 measures), and the *Audit Process Risk Mitigation Tree*© (30 measures). Part IV elaborately describes the 66 individual risk mitigation measures and matches the risk mitigations to the risk categories in a risk mitigation matrix.

Figure 1 - Book Structure

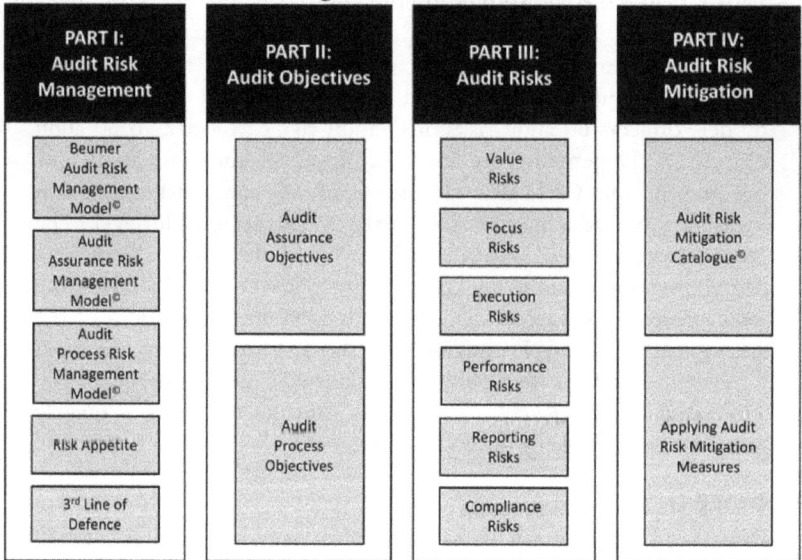

PART I: Audit Risk Management	PART II: Audit Objectives	PART III: Audit Risks	PART IV: Audit Risk Mitigation
Beumer Audit Risk Management Model©	Audit Assurance Objectives	Value Risks	Audit Risk Mitigation Catalogue©
Audit Assurance Risk Management Model©		Focus Risks	
Audit Process Risk Management Model©		Execution Risks	
		Performance Risks	
Risk Appetite	Audit Process Objectives	Reporting Risks	Applying Audit Risk Mitigation Measures
3rd Line of Defence		Compliance Risks	

PART I
-
AUDIT
RISK
MANAGEMENT

Figure 2 – PART I: Audit Risk Management

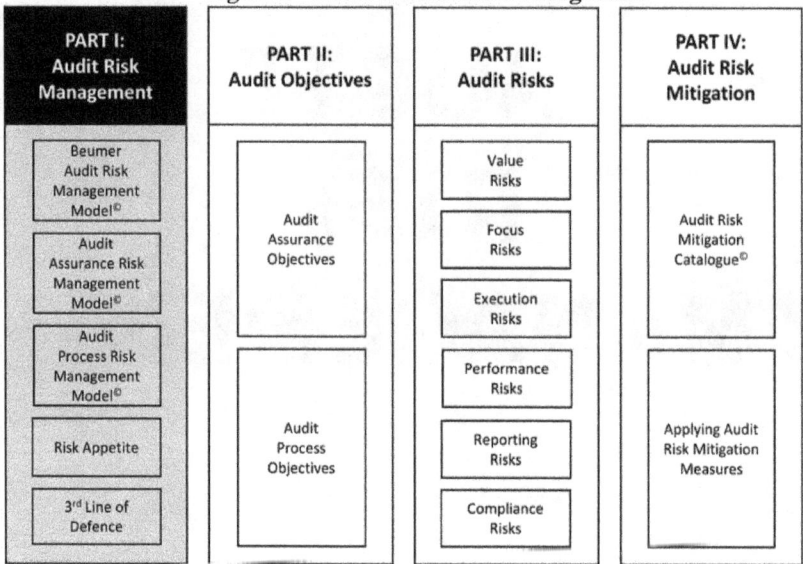

PART I: Audit Risk Management	PART II: Audit Objectives	PART III: Audit Risks	PART IV: Audit Risk Mitigation
Beumer Audit Risk Management Model©		Value Risks	
Audit Assurance Risk Management Model©	Audit Assurance Objectives	Focus Risks	Audit Risk Mitigation Catalogue©
		Execution Risks	
Audit Process Risk Management Model©		Performance Risks	
Risk Appetite	Audit Process Objectives	Reporting Risks	Applying Audit Risk Mitigation Measures
3rd Line of Defence		Compliance Risks	

Where were the Auditors?

Major corporate scandals 2010-2016

VOLKSWAGEN EMISSIONS SCANDAL

September 2015 – The US Environmental Protection Agency caught VW cheating on diesel emissions tests to falsely pass the maximum allowed levels. Diesel models had software installed to fraudulently show that the cars were more environmental friendly than they actually were.

More than 11 million cars had to be refitted, regulatory fines amounted to more than $15 billion, civil and criminal suits cost further billions. High profile managers and the CEO were dismissed.

Possible audit risks:
- Focus risk
- Overlooking issues risk
- Execution risk

FIFA CORRUPTION SCANDAL

May 2015 – The FBI indicted the FIFA organisation and officials with racketeering, fraud, corruption, and with paying millions of dollars in bribes to influence FIFA elections, locations for hosting the World Cup, sponsorship contracts, broadcasting rights, and more.

Possible audit risks:
- Focus risk
- Overlooking issues risk
- Support risk

BP OIL SPILL SCANDAL

April 2010 – The Deepwater Horizon rig explosion caused the largest environmental disaster of the 21st Century. Oil and gas producer BP had the worst health, safety and environment practices, which caused damages and cost by far exceeding $25 billion, and destructed shareholder value by more than $100 billion.

Possible audit risks:
- Focus risk
- Overlooking issues risk
- Support risk

YAHOO HACKING SCANDAL OF 1 BILLION USER ACCOUNTS

December 2016 – Yahoo disclosed that a data breach exposed the private information of more than 1 billion user accounts. It related to a theft of names, email addresses, telephone numbers, birthdates, and unrecognisable passwords, as well as encrypted and non-encrypted security questions and answers.

WELLS FARGO SCANDAL OF FAKE ACCOUNTS

September 2016 – Over the period 2011-2016, Retail Banking employees created 1.5 million phoney deposit accounts and issued 0.5 million fake credit cards, without the knowledge or permission of the related customers. Employees resorted to fraud in order to meet challenging growth quotas.
The bank paid $185 million in fines and fired 5'300 employees.

Possible audit risks:
- Focus risk
- Overlooking issues risk

OLYMPUS ACCOUNTING AND BRIBERY SCANDAL

October 2011 - Olympus hid $1.7 billion in losses over a period of 13 years and admitted to paying kickbacks and foreign bribery.

The company paid more than $0.5 billion to settle criminal and civil investigations.

Possible audit risks:
- Focus risk
- Overlooking issues risk

PETROBRAS CORRUPTION SCANDAL

March 2014 – Executives and key management of Brazil's state-owned Oil & Gas Company were accused of bribery of officials as well as siphoning off money for their own use. In criminal investigations, more than 80 managers and politicians were charged with money laundering and bribery of more than $8 billion.

Possible audit risks:
- Focus risk
- Overlooking issues risk
- Support risk

LIBOR RIGGING SCANDAL

June 2012 – Criminal investigations into the manipulation of interest rates spread to 10 countries and involved more than 20 major banks. Total fines reached more than $10 billion.

Possible audit risks:
- Focus risk
- Overlooking issues risk
- Execution risk

Possible audit risks:
- Focus risk
- Overlooking issues risk
- Execution risk

Where were the internal auditors?

These eight examples represent some of the major scandals, bribery, corruption, fraud, and non-compliance cases in the period 2010-2016. In each of these cases, you can rightfully ask "Where were the internal auditors?" The answers to this question are manifold:

- Focus risk: the audit function did not have the topics in their audit universe, as other assurance providers covered these topics:
  - External audit: Olympus
  - Compliance and EHS departments: BP, VW
  - IT security: Yahoo
- Focus/execution risk: the audit function did have the topics in their audit universe, but:
  - did not assess the risks correctly: VW, BP, Petrobras, Wells Fargo, Yahoo
  - did not understand the transactions: Libor, Olympus
  - did not have an appropriate focus: Petrobras, FIFA, BP, Yahoo
  - did not have the right auditor skills: could be all of them
  - had scope limitations or insufficient support: FIFA, Petrobras
- Execution risk: the audit function did audit the related topics, but:
  - did not identify the issues: Libor, Wells Fargo, Yahoo
  - did not agree with management on effective risk mitigation: BP, Yahoo
  - did not follow-up on the risk reduction: BP, Yahoo
  - management hid the problems: Olympus, Petrobras
- Support risk: the audit function did raise the relevant issues, but:
  - management did not support the audit function: FIFA
  - management did not implement risk mitigation: BP, Yahoo

We will never know the real reasons for these companies' audit functions inability to successfully identify these issues and have management mitigate those risks. For the internal audit functions of these companies, it is already too late. Their effectiveness will probably have been seriously questioned, and this might have resulted in the dismissal of the CAE, downsizing or upsizing of the audit function, combined with a refocus of the audit function's strategy and objectives. However, for your company's audit function a similar scandal can be avoided. The strategic audit risk management model presented in this book comes to the rescue, and provides practical guidance for preventing and reducing such audit function risks.

Focus, focus, focus

When you analyse the audit risks of these eight cases, a clear trend can be identified. In all these scandals two audit risks stand out: the focus risk and the risk of overlooking significant issues. These two risks are predominantly present in the risk profile of each and every audit function, irrespective of the type of organisation, the industry, the size of the audit function or the geographic location. The focus risk can be present at the audit function level as well as the audit engagement level, whereas the risk of overlooking significant issues applies to the audit engagement level only. It is clear that mitigating the focus risk and the risk of overlooking significant issues are the major contributors to safeguarding the success of any audit function.

Support risk is the next dominant risk for the audit function. In case management and the board do not (or insufficiently) support the internal audit function, it will be difficult for the CAE to ensure the necessary execution of the annual audit plan and the audit engagements focus on the value-added topics. Mitigating the support risk is, therefore, a strict requirement for achieving the customer value proposition of any audit function.

No risk, no reward

The primary objective of the audit function must be to add value. This means that the CAE must be value driven, as she aims to mitigate the business risks that may keep the company from reaching its objectives. Some CAEs' first objective, however, is to limit the risks of the audit function. They are driven by their personal risk-aversion, by creating a comfort zone, and not do anything that may antagonise management or put them in the spotlight (low risk-appetite). However, the CAE needs to be willing to take some risks to achieve bigger audit results. Had the internal audit functions in the above examples taken some bigger risks in addressing the scandalous topics, perhaps they could have prevented these from occurring, or they could have been timely mitigated before being exposed. The CAE needs to understand her audit risks and manage them, to achieve big audit results.

The CAE can provide significant added value to the company, while at the same time reducing her audit risks. She can create a win-win (for the company and herself), but she needs to follow the guidance in this book to realise this. Her appetite for the added value of the internal audit function must lead the way, as the audit risks are a result of the selection of the audit engagements that add to that value. It should not be done the other way around, by letting her appetite for the audit risks determine which added value audits are going to be undertaken. The CAE must find the appropriate trade-off between the level of the audit risk and the potential for generating audit value.

Why manage audit risks?

To be able to add value to the organisation, the CAE must ensure that she does not have:

- a lack of support from the process owners, local management, executive management and the board, as a result of which the board limits the approved resources and the audit products are not utilised.

- a mismatch between the risk profile and the main business strategies and objectives of the company or subject matter, and the focus of the annual audit plan or the audit engagement.

- a negative input – output ratio, if the costs of the audit function and the audit engagements are considered to be too high compared to the value generated.

To be able to add value to the organisation, the CAE must ensure that she does not issue:

- an unqualified, satisfactory, audit opinion/report, without reporting any significant issues, whereas significant issues do exist in the audited subject matter.

- a qualified, unsatisfactory, audit opinion/report, pointing out significant issues, whereas the issues are either not significant, or do not exist in the audited subject matter.

- a full scope audit opinion/report on the audited subject matter, whereas she should not issue such an opinion/report based on significant limitations in the audit scope or the audit execution.

Understanding, identifying, measuring, and proactively managing the audit risks are necessary for ensuring the audit function's and the CAE's success in the company.

The next chapter introduces the *Beumer Audit Risk Management Model*© creating a unique new framework for managing the audit risks and preventing your company's name to be included in the listing of "where were the auditors?".

Audit Risk Management

Beumer Audit Risk Management Model©

The *Beumer Audit Risk Management Model©* captures the quintessence of managing the audit risks in an innovative way. Through its holistic approach, the model can be used with any risk management standard, such as COSO-ERM or ISO 31000. Use the following guidance for the interpretation of the model:

- The risk management flow captured in the top-left quadrant (with the light-grey colour background) shows the 1st and 2nd lines of defence (in the management processes integrated risk management and control systems respectively the separate functions that overlay them, such as risk management and compliance). The risk management process flows from the company objectives, the board's risk appetite, the 1st and 2nd lines of defence, to the resulting company or subject matter risks, are not discussed in this book, as these relate to management's risk management processes (as opposed to the audit function's risk management processes).

- The other three quadrants show the risk management of the 3rd line of defence itself: the audit function.

- Similar to the company's risk management process, the audit function's risk management process starts with the audit function objectives, against which the risks need to be measured.

- The CAE's risk appetite determines the level of internal process risks that he is seeking to maintain in the pursuit of his audit function objectives. For the audit assurance on the company's risks, however, the risk appetite of the board is decisive.

- The audit function structure, organisation, processes and procedures act as the 3rd line of defence. The understanding and managing of the audit function's inherent risks and control risks enable the CAE to reduce the occurrence of the audit function risks.

- From the audit function's risk management perspective, the audit function risks (to the achievement of the audit function objectives) are captured in the audit function's risk universe. This risk universe can be divided into two categories: the audit assurance risks and the audit process risks.

- The audit assurance risks arise from applying the audit function risks of value, focus and execution to the company's risk universe.

- The audit process risks arise from applying the audit function risks of performance, reporting and compliance to the audit assurance activities.

- The audit assurance risk mitigation (in order to achieve the desirable level of residual assurance risk) depends on the risk appetite of the board, whereas the audit process risk mitigation (in order to achieve the desirable level of residual process risk) depends on the risk appetite of the CAE.

- The residual audit assurance risks reflect the level of risk consistent with the risk appetite of the board.

- The residual audit process risks reflect the level of risk consistent with the risk appetite of the CAE.

The *Beumer Audit Risk Management Model*© shows that the audit function is exposed to two main sources of the audit risks:

1. The assurance operations of the audit function. These assurance operations are linked to the objectives of improving the company by helping the company achieve its objectives. They are the drivers for the audit risk management.

2. The internal operations of the audit function. These internal operations are linked to the objectives of running an efficient and effective audit function. They are the enablers for the audit risk management.

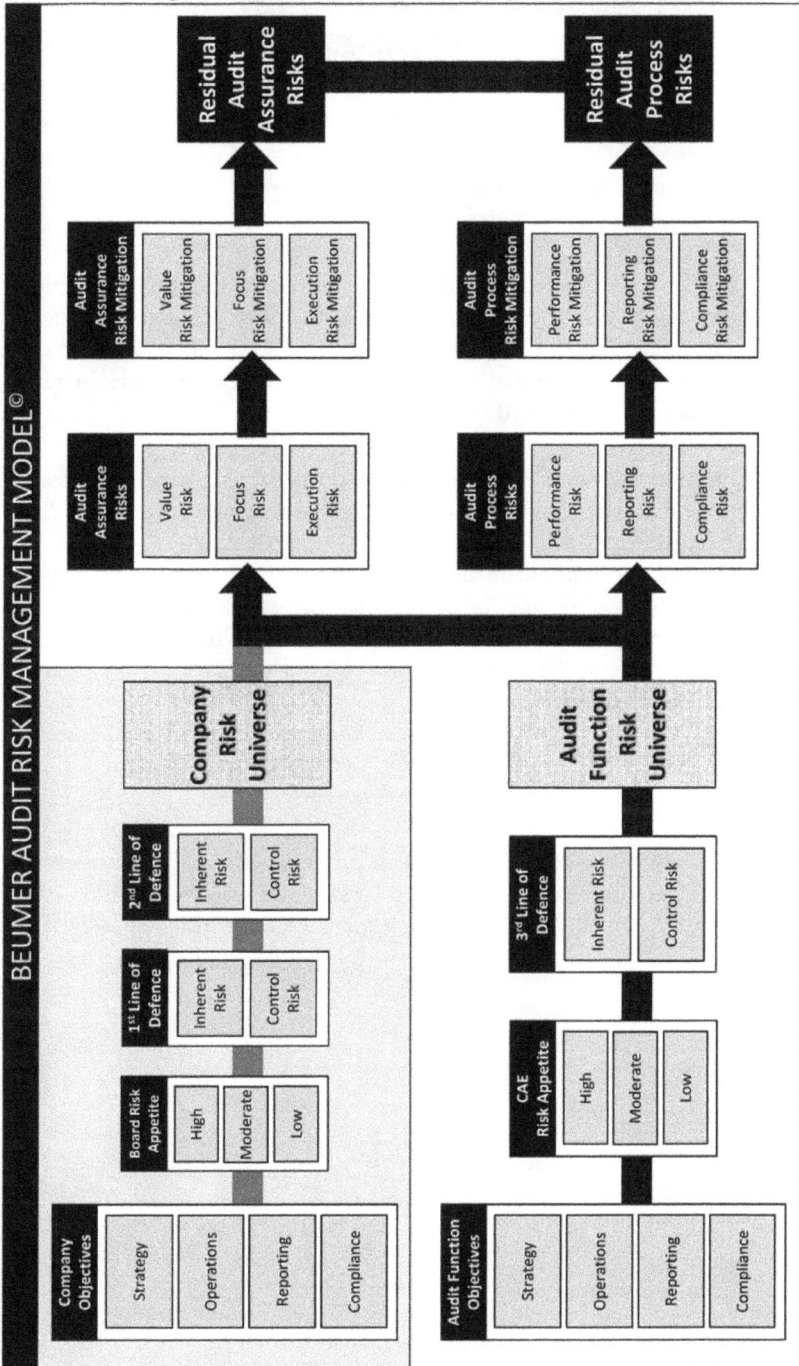

Figure 3 – Beumer Audit Risk Management Model©

Audit Assurance Risk Management Model©

Consistent with the *Beumer Audit Risk Management Model©*, the audit assurance risks reflect the application of the audit function's value risks, focus risks and execution risks to the company's risk universe. Use the following guidance for the interpretation of this model:

- The 14 audit assurance objectives represent the audit function's strategies to create value for the board and management, ensuring an appropriate focus of the annual audit plan and the audit engagements, and executing the annual planning and the audit engagements in such a way that value is created.

- The audit assurance risks show the 33 potential risks to which the audit function can be exposed. The level of the risk exposures depends on several factors:
  - o The risk appetite of the CAE.
  - o The level of the inherent risk and control risk of the audit function (driven by the risk appetite of the CAE).
  - o The size of the audit function's risk universe.
  - o The risk appetite of the board.
  - o The level of the inherent risk and control risk of the 1st and 2nd lines of defence (driven by the risk appetite of the board).
  - o The size of the company's risk universe.

- The audit assurance risk mitigations offer 36 risk mitigation measures to reduce the value risks, focus risks and execution risks to an acceptable level. This level is determined by the risk appetite of the board.

Figure 4 – Audit Assurance Risk Management Model©

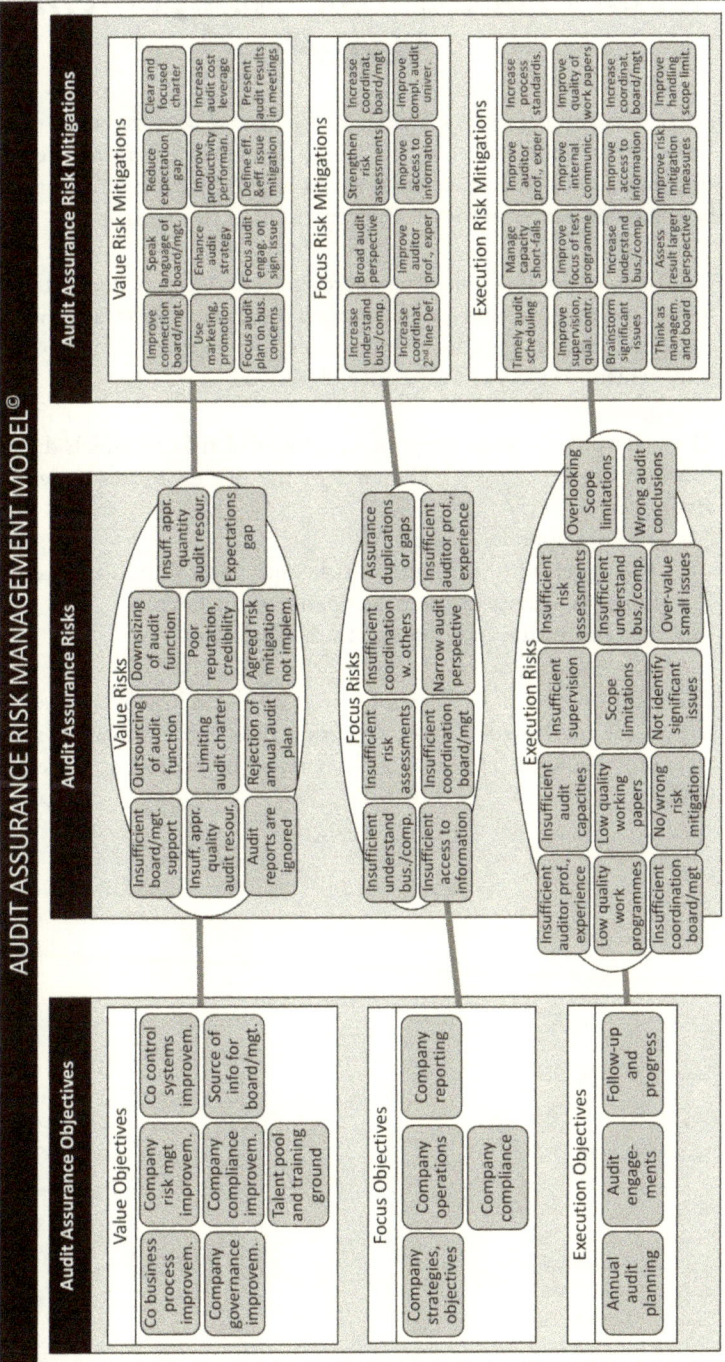

AUDIT ASSURANCE RISK MANAGEMENT MODEL©

Audit Assurance Objectives

Value Objectives
- Co business process improvem.
- Company risk mgt improvem.
- Co control systems improvem.
- Company governance improvem.
- Company compliance improvem.
- Source of info for board/mgt.
- Talent pool and training ground

Focus Objectives
- Company strategies, objectives
- Company operations
- Company reporting
- Company compliance

Execution Objectives
- Annual audit planning
- Audit engagements
- Follow-up and progress

Audit Assurance Risks

Value Risks
- Insufficient board/mgt. support
- Insuff. appr. quality audit resour.
- Audit reports are ignored
- Outsourcing of audit function
- Limiting audit charter
- Rejection of annual audit plan
- Downsizing of audit function
- Poor reputation, credibility
- Agreed risk mitigation not implem.
- Insuff. appr. quantity audit resour.
- Expectations gap

Focus Risks
- Insufficient understand bus./comp.
- Insufficient access to information
- Insufficient risk assessments
- Insufficient coordination board/mgt
- Insufficient coordination w. others
- Narrow audit perspective
- Assurance duplications or gaps
- Insufficient auditor prof. experience

Execution Risks
- Insufficient auditor prof., experience
- Insufficient coordination board/mgt
- Low quality work programmes
- Insufficient audit capacities
- Low quality working papers
- No/wrong risk mitigation
- Insufficient supervision
- Scope limitations
- Not identify significant issues
- Insufficient risk assessments
- Insufficient understand bus./comp.
- Over-value small issues
- Overlooking Scope limitations
- Wrong audit conclusions

Audit Assurance Risk Mitigations

Value Risk Mitigations
- Improve connection board/mgt.
- Speak language of board/mgt.
- Reduce expectation gap
- Clear and focused charter
- Use marketing, promotion
- Enhance audit strategy
- Improve productivity performan.
- Increase audit cost leverage
- Focus audit plan on bus. concerns
- Define eff. & eff. issue mitigation
- Focus audit engage. on sign. issue
- Present audit results in meetings

Focus Risk Mitigations
- Increase understand bus./comp.
- Broad audit perspective
- Strengthen risk assessments
- Increase coordinat. board/mgt
- Increase coordinat. 2nd line Def
- Improve auditor prof., exper
- Improve access to information
- Improve compl. audit univer.

Execution Risk Mitigations
- Timely audit scheduling
- Manage capacity short-falls
- Improve auditor prof., exper
- Increase process standards.
- Improve supervision, qual. contr.
- Improve focus of test programme
- Improve internal communic.
- Improve quality of work papers
- Brainstorm significant issues
- Increase understand bus./comp.
- Improve access to information
- Increase coordinat. board/mgt
- Think as managem. and board
- Assess result larger perspective
- Improve risk mitigation measures
- Improve handling scope limit.

Audit Process Risk Management Model©

Consistent with the *Beumer Audit Risk Management Model©*, the audit process risks reflect the application of the audit function's performance risks, reporting risks and compliance risks to the audit function's risk universe. Use the following guidance for the interpretation of this model:

- The 16 audit process objectives represent the audit function's strategies to run an efficient and effective audit function. These are the audit function's internal process objectives that need to support the achievement of the audit assurance objectives.

- The audit process risks show the 27 potential risks to which the audit function can be exposed. The level of the risk exposures depends on several factors:
  o The risk appetite of the CAE.
  o The level of the inherent risk and control risk of the audit function (driven by the risk appetite of the CAE).
  o The size of the audit function's risk universe.

- The audit process risk mitigations offer 30 risk mitigation measures to reduce the performance risks, reporting risks and compliance risks to an acceptable level. This level is determined by the risk appetite of the CAE.

Figure 5 – Audit Process Risk Management Model©

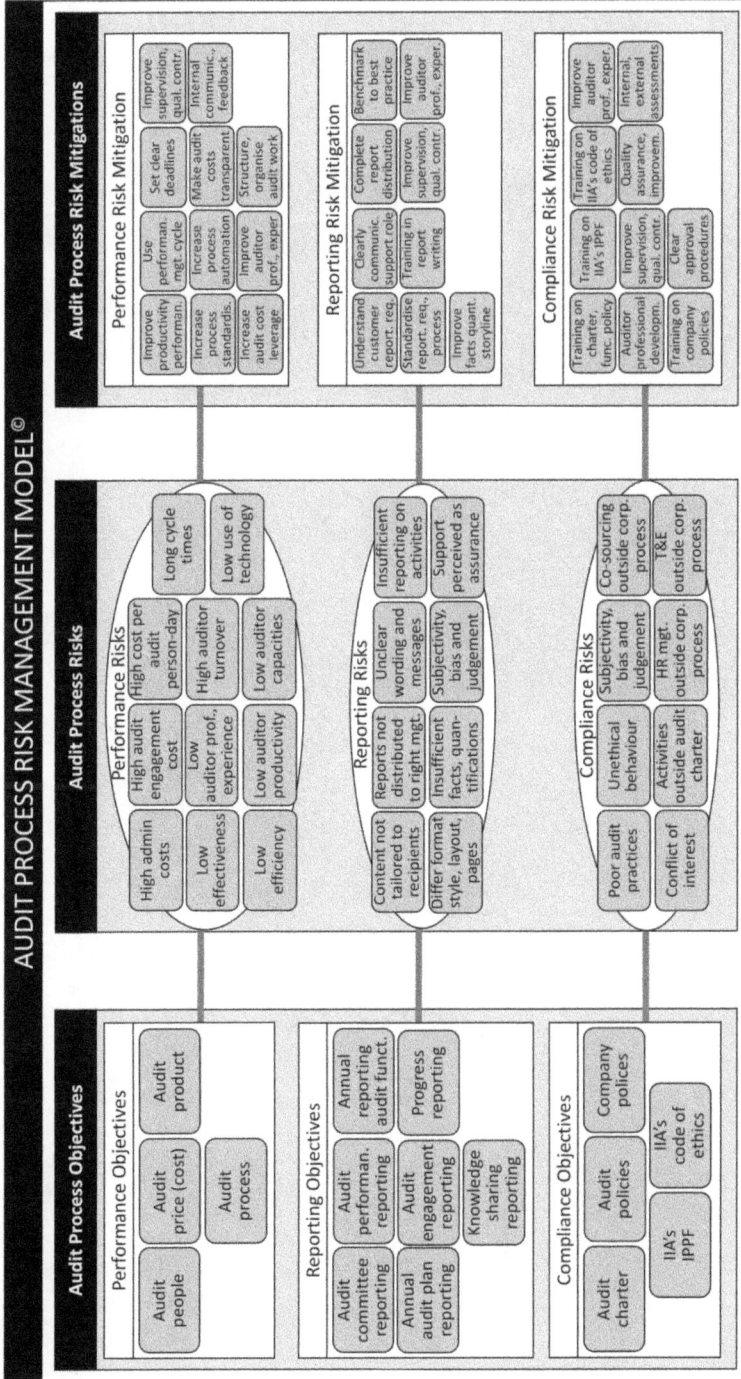

AUDIT PROCESS RISK MANAGEMENT MODEL©

Audit Process Objectives

Performance Objectives

- Audit people
- Audit price (cost)
- Audit product
- Audit process

Reporting Objectives

- Audit committee reporting
- Audit performan. reporting
- Annual reporting audit funct.
- Annual audit plan reporting
- Audit engagement reporting
- Progress reporting
- Knowledge sharing reporting

Compliance Objectives

- Audit charter
- Audit policies
- Company policies
- IIA's IPPF
- IIA's code of ethics

Audit Process Risks

Performance Risks

- High admin costs
- High audit engagement cost
- High cost per audit person-day
- Long cycle times
- Low effectiveness
- Low auditor prof., experience
- High auditor turnover
- Low use of technology
- Low efficiency
- Low auditor productivity
- Low auditor capacities

Reporting Risks

- Content not tailored to recipients
- Reports not distributed to right mgt.
- Unclear wording and messages
- Insufficient reporting on activities
- Differ format style, layout, pages
- Insufficient facts, quantifications
- Subjectivity, bias and judgement
- Support perceived as assurance

Compliance Risks

- Poor audit practices
- Unethical behaviour
- Subjectivity, bias and judgement
- Co-sourcing outside corp. process
- Conflict of interest
- Activities outside audit charter
- HR mgt. outside corp. process
- T&E outside corp. process

Audit Process Risk Mitigations

Performance Risk Mitigation

- Improve productivity performan.
- Use performan. mgt. cycle
- Set clear deadlines
- Improve supervision, qual. contr.
- Increase process standards.
- Increase process automation
- Make audit costs transparent
- Internal communic., feedback
- Increase audit cost leverage
- Improve auditor prof., exper
- Structure, organise audit work

Reporting Risk Mitigation

- Understand customer report. req.
- Clearly communic. report. req.
- Complete report distribution
- Benchmark to best practice
- Standardise report. req., process
- Training in report writing
- Improve supervision, qual. contr.
- Improve auditor prof., exper.
- Improve facts quant. storyline

Compliance Risk Mitigation

- Training on charter, func. policy
- Training on IIA's IPPF
- Training on IIA's code of ethics
- Improve auditor prof. exper.
- Auditor professional developm.
- Improve supervision, qual. contr.
- Quality assurance, improvem.
- Internal, external assessments
- Training on company policies
- Clear approval procedures

Risk Appetite

Definitions

In the risk management language, there are several key words used to express risk behaviour:

- Risk attitude: the general behaviour towards risks: risk averse, risk neutral or risk seeking.
- Risk capacity: the total amount of risk that a company is able to accept.
- Risk tolerance: the total amount of risk that a company is willing to accept.
- Risk appetite: the total amount of risk that a company is seeking to accept.
- Risk target: the optimum amount of risk that the company is aiming for.
- Gross risk: the level (impact and likelihood) of the risk before treatment.
- Risk treatment: acceptance, avoidance, transfer, or reduction of the risk.
- Net risk or residual risk: the level (impact and likelihood) of the risk after risk treatment.

Figure 6 – Key Risk Terminology

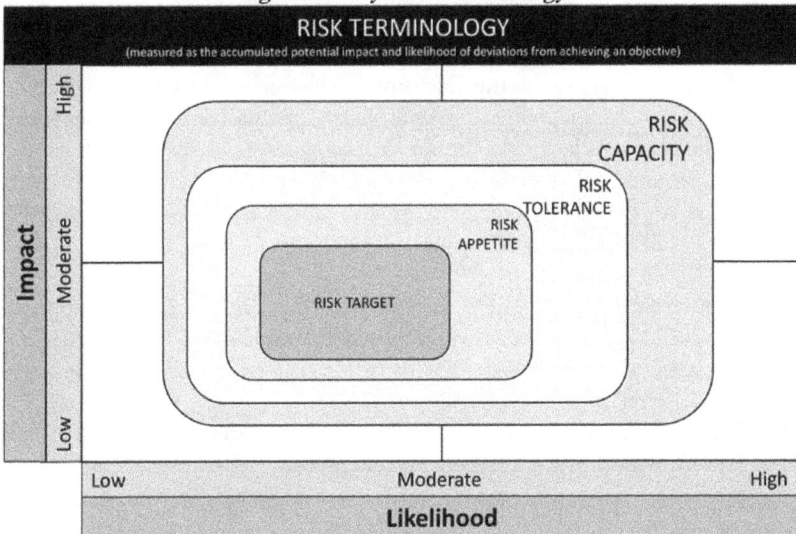

CAE's risk appetite

Consistent with the *Beumer Audit Risk Management Model*©, the CAE's risk appetite plays an important role in setting the level of the risks in the 3rd line of defence.

The CAE's risk appetite represents the level of risk that she is seeking to accept in pursuit of the audit function strategies and objectives. It is neither efficient nor economical to have a 100 percent risk prevention or to reduce the audit function process risks to zero by fully deploying all required risk mitigating measures. In effect this means the following:

- The audit function's standard internal processes must be able to prevent the standard risks towards achieving the audit strategies and objectives for the operation of the audit function. It is the risk appetite of the CAE that defines at which level this standard is. Is the CAE more risk averse, then the standard internal audit processes will be of a higher quality, aiming for a higher level of risk prevention. Is the CAE seeking to allow a certain level of risk (in order to enhance the efficiency and effectiveness of her internal processes), then the quality standard of risk prevention may be lower compared to a CAE who has a low risk appetite.

- Whatever the standard level of the risk prevention, there will always be risks that slip through the safety net (as a 100 percent prevention is neither desirable nor economical). These risks then relate to situations which are non-standard. These non-standard situations may be caused by: failure to correctly apply the standard level of risk prevention; new auditors; changes in the board or management; new company strategies; changes in the customer value proposition; an increasing expectations gap; increasing compliance requirements, and so forth. These non-standard risks require risk mitigation, which depends on the risk appetite of the CAE. She will have to initiate specific risk mitigating measures to reduce the risk to the level of the residual risk that is still within her risk appetite.

For the internal processes, it is fair to state that the CAE's risk appetite drives both the level of risk prevention and the level of risk mitigation, and thus the level of residual risk that is (accepted) contained in these audit function's internal processes.
This situation is different for the audit assurance processes. Here the board determines the level of the acceptable residual risk.

Board's risk appetite

The risk appetite of the board plays a major role in setting the level of the risk assurance that these key customers want to obtain from the audit function. The risk appetite of the board (usually in congruence with the risk appetite of the CEO and executive management) determines the level of the residual risk that they are pursuing in their quest for achieving the company's strategies and objectives.

The assurance role of the audit department has the objective to assess whether the 1st and 2nd lines of defence have identified and are managing (accepting, avoiding, transferring or reducing) the risks contained in the deployment of the board approved business strategies. This assurance role has several risk appetite related aspects:

- The identification of the company (gross) risks as part of the annual audit planning and the execution of the audit engagements. Based on the risk-based audit assurance approach (I refer to *Driving Audit Value, Volumes I* and *III*), the audit function will usually start by trying to identify the potentially high risks and then work its way down to the potentially moderate and low risks. A single low risk may be acceptable, but an accumulation of low risks may point to systemic risks or to a risk accumulation of an unacceptable level (beyond the risk appetite of the board). This is why it is recommendable not to limit the risk identification to the potential high and moderate risks only. Three factors influence the decision how far down to go into the low risks:
  - o The risk appetite of the board.
  - o The potential for identifying systemic risks or unacceptable risk accumulations.
  - o The audit efficiency and economy, as well as the effectiveness in identifying potential deviations from the company's objectives.

Take the example of the VW emissions scandal at the beginning of this book. The identification of the problem surely started with one technical compliance test showing a deviation from the regulations. In itself, the result of this one test was probably a low risk with a low impact. However, when multiplied by the millions of cars, the impact becomes enormous.

- Management's mitigation of the company risks (1st and 2nd lines of defence): once the company risks have been identified, it is the responsibility of the audit function to assess management's risk mitigation measures. In this respect, the risk appetite of the board has a strong influence: management should be mitigating the risks to a level that is within the risk appetite of the board.

- Further lowering of the residual risk: in the case that management was not aware of the risk, was aware of the risk but failed to initiate risk mitigation, or initiated insufficient risk mitigation, it is within the assurance responsibility of the audit function to agree with management additional risk mitigating actions. These actions must reduce the residual risk to a level that is within the risk appetite of the board. It is then in the judgement of the audit function, in coordination with management, to determine the appropriate (cost-effective and efficient) risk mitigation measures. This is why the CAE must have a good understanding of the risk appetite of the board. In-depth discussions with the chairman of the audit committee may provide a strong contribution to such an understanding.

For example: the board requires the company's operations to be fully compliant with the laws (risk appetite: zero). In a review of logistical operations, the auditor identifies that the company received governmental approval to maintain a bonded warehouse. The following risk scenarios are possible:

- o Local management was not aware of the customs requirements, or failed to implement any of the requirements that allow the bonded warehouse to be maintained. The 1st and 2nd lines of defence did not identify the risk of non-compliance, hence, significant risks of non-compliance, penalties and disallowing of the concept exist. The auditor will have to agree with management all the necessary risk mitigation measures for bringing the company into full compliance with the customs requirements.
- o Local management implemented the administrative separation of the goods in their bonded and non-bonded warehouses. However, they did not physically separate the goods: they are mixed within the warehouse storage. The auditor will have to agree with management that they physically separate the goods consistent with the requirements of the customs authorities.

- In my personal experience, it happens that management shows a higher risk appetite than the board. Management may be driven by stretched goals, for which they may also stretch their risk appetite. They may seek higher risks in order to achieve the challenging objectives. The audit assurance activities play an important role for the board in terms of identifying such situations and adjusting the risk levels back to the board's risk appetite.

For example: The board set a stretched sales target of $100 million. According to the sales forecasts, management expects to realise $85 million in sales. These $85 million are based on a full compliance of the sales activities with the code of conduct. Management estimates that they can achieve an additional $20 million in sales when they approach potential customers in their markets in Pakistan, Venezuela, Saudi Arabia and Vietnam. Management is aware that these transactions can only be realised when they offer the customers, or their intermediary agents, some additional incentives that are not reconcilable with the code of conduct. They stretch their risk appetite for compliance risks to achieve the sales target. The VW emissions scandal is a similar example.

- It can also happen that management shows a lower risk appetite than the board. This lower risk appetite may actually endanger the achievement of the company's strategies and objectives (after all, the expression is "no risk, no reward"). The impact on the audit assurance risks of the audit function could be that the auditor should identify additional actions for management to achieve their objectives. This then goes in the direction of recommending to management that they take additional risks (contained in new activities) for achieving the goals.

- The completeness of the identification of the company (gross) risks cannot be a goal of the audit function:
  - o During the annual audit planning, the audit function has the goal to obtain a materiality-based risk profile of the company, the comprehensive overview of the most significant risks that may prevent the company from achieving its objectives (company risk universe). This means that such a risk profile can never be complete, as it focuses on the most material risks, with the biggest exposures (for example the top 30 risks).
  - o The audit function has resource restrictions, meaning that the annual audit plan will be able to cover a certain portion of the company's risk universe (the top risks, based on the risk-based approach), but can never cover all company risks. This would be neither efficient nor economical as the cost of the audit assurance might then be higher than the risk exposure that is being assessed. The audit function's assurance work is an add-on to the 1st and 2nd lines of defence. Therefore, in combination with the risk appetite of the board, the audit coverage restriction is well acceptable.
  - o During the audit engagements, the audit function has the goal to review the materiality-based risk profile of the subject matter.

This means that such a risk profile can never be complete, as it focuses on the most material risks, with the biggest exposures.

Under the perspective of the customer value proposition, the board's risk appetite, and the 1st and 2nd lines of defence, the risk coverage of the audit function does not have to be complete. The customer value proposition should result in a focus on the top risks and the risk management by the two other lines of defence. The board's risk appetite may allow a certain level of residual risk to exist (as risks do not need to be mitigated to a zero impact and likelihood). This means that low risks may stay outside the scope of work of the audit function.

Impact of risk appetite on risk mitigation

The following model provides guidance for keeping the (residual) audit risks at an acceptable level. What constitutes an acceptable level of residual audit risk (after risk mitigation) for the audit activities depends on the risk appetite of the CAE and the board. The model is useful for managing and mitigating the risks relating to not achieving the target audit value (i.e. not achieving the customer's expectations or the audit function's value proposition):

Figure 7 – Impact of Risk Appetite on Risk Mitigation

	Audit Risk is		Risk Appetite is		Audit Risk Mitigation should be
	High		High		Moderate
IF	High	AND	Low	THEN	High
	Low		High		Low
	Low		Low		Moderate

3ʳᵈ Line of Defence

Inherent and control risks

Consistent with the *Beumer Audit Risk Management Model©*, the audit function's structure, risk management, governance, control systems, policies, procedures and processes must act as a line of defence against the risks of not achieving the audit function objectives. These management tools must enable the running of an efficient and effective audit function.

An efficient and effective audit function will ensure that the audit function objectives can be achieved. In this respect, they serve to prevent the risks of non-efficiency and non-effectiveness. The level of risk prevention can be determined by assessing the audit function's inherent risks and control risks. The lower the inherent and control risks, the higher the risk prevention. The higher the inherent risks and control risks, the lower the risk prevention. The definitions are as follows:

- Audit function inherent risk: the risk that the audit function or the audit engagement structures, complexity, or audit management itself are inadequate to prevent significant deviations from achieving the audit strategies and objectives.

- Audit function control risk: the risk that the control and risk management systems of the audit function or of the audit engagement are inadequate to prevent significant deviations from achieving the audit strategies and objectives.

Once the CAE understands the risk profile and the risk level of the internal processes, she is able to determine what type and level of risks the audit function may be exposed to, and she is able to select the appropriate approach for mitigating these audit risks.

Audit function process maturity level

If the audit function has a high level of process maturity, the CAE will have processes in place that continuously monitor and improve the quality of the audit function processes and procedures. In such cases the control risk will be low. To the contrary, if the audit function has a low level of process maturity, there will be a significant scope for improving the audit processes and procedures. In such cases the control risk will be high, and it is the

CAE's responsibility to maintain a quality assurance and improvement programme to reduce the control risk to an acceptable level, thereby increasing the audit risk prevention. The higher the control risks, the lower the maturity level, and vice versa.

In the next sections, a model is presented to determine the maturity level of the audit function's structures, risk management and control processes for the purpose of assessing the level of risk prevention.

Both the sections for the inherent risk and the control risk have the following structure: they start with a definition of the risk, followed by examples, an analysis of the risk drivers, and finally guidance for assessing the level of the risk.

The chapter is completed with the *Audit Function Risk Indicators Model©*, summarising the inherent and control risk indicators for assessing the level of the 3rd line of defence.

Audit function inherent risk

Figure 8 – Six Indicators of Audit Function Inherent Risk

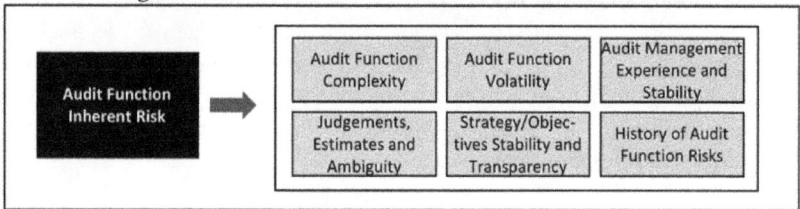

Definition

The inherent risk of the audit function is the probability that the audit function's structures, complexity, audit management or the auditors, are inadequate in preventing significant deviations from achieving the audit strategies and objectives. It is the risk of insufficient audit performance, caused by the set-up of the audit function.

The CAE must manage (reduce) the audit function inherent risk in order to increase the audit risk prevention capacity of the audit function. The lower the inherent risk, the lower the probability of audit risks occurring.

Examples

The audit function inherent risk may be high in the large conglomerate companies, where the audit function is spread over 10 business divisions, each active in different industries, with 300 staff auditors and 80 audit managers, spread over 25 worldwide locations.

Risk Drivers

The following risk drivers have a significant influence on the level of the inherent risk, and the higher each of these elements, the higher the inherent risk:

- The degree of non-transparency and frequency of change of audit function structures, audit strategies and audit objectives, and the level of difficulty of having the entire audit team work towards one common audit strategy.
- The frequency of changes of the audit staff, audit management and the CAE.
- The degree of complexity and geographical spread of the audit function.
- The level of ambiguity and uncertainty within the underlying audit processes, and audit management's inexperience in managing these complexities.
- The degree of estimations and judgement that the auditors, audit management and the CAE need to make to put together the annual audit plan and to complete the audit engagements.

Determining risk levels

The audit function has a high inherent risk when: the CAE frequently changes; the audit strategies and objectives frequently change; the audit function is spread over many geographic locations; the audit function has many layers between the CAE and the field auditors; the audit engagements involve subject matters with highly judgemental content; the auditors, audit management and the CAE are inexperienced.

The audit function has a low inherent risk when: the CAE has a consistent, clear and transparent audit strategy; the CAE and audit staff are experienced; the entire function is based in one main office location; the audit function has a lean and flat structure.

The higher the inherent risk, the lower the risk prevention.

Audit function control risk

Figure 9 – Six Indicators of Audit Function Control Risk

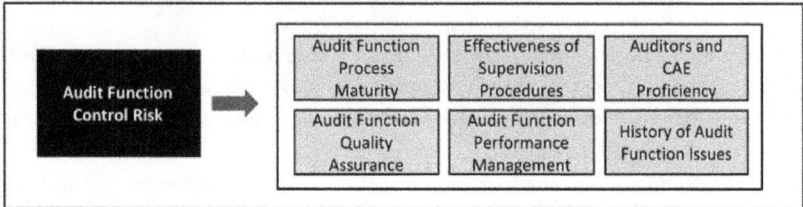

| Audit Function Control Risk | Audit Function Process Maturity | Effectiveness of Supervision Procedures | Auditors and CAE Proficiency |
| | Audit Function Quality Assurance | Audit Function Performance Management | History of Audit Function Issues |

Definition

The control risk of the audit function is the probability that the control and risk management systems of the audit function are inadequate in preventing significant deviations from achieving the audit strategies and objectives. If the audit function has no, weak or failing internal control and risk management systems, the control risk may be substantial. The higher the control risk, the higher the likelihood that the audit function will incur audit risks.

The CAE must manage (reduce) the audit function control risk in order to increase the audit risk prevention capacity of the audit function. The lower the control risk, the lower the probability of audit risks occurring.

Examples

High control risks may exist in an audit function that has no standardised processes and procedures, only uses generic work programmes, has no supervision processes or has auditors and a CAE who are not professionally qualified.

Risk drivers

The following risk drivers have a significant influence on the level of the control risk, and the lower each of these elements, the higher the control risk:

- The level of formalisation and the extensiveness of the audit function processes and quality control procedures.
- The extent of stability and consistent application of the audit control and risk management processes;
- The effectiveness of the internal audit supervision and quality control processes over the audit engagements and the annual audit planning.
- The extensiveness of the audit engagement work programmes.
- The level of proficiency of the auditor/audit manager/CAE.

Determining risk levels

The audit function has a high control risk when: the CAE has no supervision and quality control processes in place; working with newly recruited inexperienced auditors; the audit testing programmes are generic, not tailored to the subject matter being audited; there is no performance management in place.

The audit function has a low control risk when: the supervision and quality control processes are formalised and effective; the CAE has qualified and experienced auditors; the audit testing programmes are tailor made to the risk profile of the subject matter; an extensive performance management is in place.

The higher the control risk, the lower the risk prevention.

Audit Function Risk Indicators Model[©]

The *Audit Function Risk Indicators Model*[©] summarises the main risk indicators for the inherent risk and control risk to quickly grasp the risks of the audit function towards the success in achieving the audit strategies and objectives. The CAE can use this model when interviewing for the job as CAE at a new company (to decide if she is willing to accept the level of risk) or for defining the risk level for her current audit function, and taking the appropriate measures to increase the risk prevention.

Figure 10 – Audit Function Risk Indicators Model©

AUDIT FUNCTION RISK INDICATORS MODEL© - 3rd Line of Defence

Control risk \ Inherent risk	Low	Moderate	High
High	• low complexity of audit function • low changing audit strategies/objectives • low frequency of audit risks • low audit management turnover • low level of audit performance management • low quality assurance, improvement programme • low audit process maturity • low proficiency and quality audit management	• medium complexity of audit function • medium changing audit strategies/objectives • medium frequency of audit risks • medium audit management turnover • low level of audit performance management • low quality assurance, improvement programme • low audit process maturity • low proficiency and quality audit management *(Medium Audit Risk Prevention)*	• high complexity of audit function • high changing audit strategies/objectives • high frequency of audit risks • high audit management turnover • low level of audit performance management • low quality assurance, improvement programme • low audit process maturity • low proficiency and quality audit management *(Low Audit Risk Prevention)*
Moderate	• low complexity of audit function • low changing audit strategies/objectives • low frequency of audit risks • low audit management turnover • medium level of audit performance management • medium quality assurance, improvement programme • medium audit process maturity • medium proficiency and quality audit management	• medium complexity of audit function • medium changing audit strategies/objectives • medium frequency of audit risks • medium audit management turnover • medium level of audit performance management • medium quality assurance, improvement programme • medium audit process maturity • medium proficiency and quality audit management	• high complexity of audit function • high changing audit strategies/objectives • high frequency of audit risks • high audit management turnover • medium level of audit performance management • medium quality assurance, improvement programme • medium audit process maturity • medium proficiency and quality audit management
Low	• low complexity of audit function • low changing audit strategies/objectives • low frequency of audit risks • low audit management turnover • high level of audit performance management • high quality assurance, improvement programme • high audit process maturity • high proficiency and quality audit management *(High Audit Risk Prevention)*	• medium complexity of audit function • medium changing audit strategies/objectives • medium frequency of audit risks • medium audit management turnover • high level of audit performance management • high quality assurance, improvement programme • high audit process maturity • high proficiency and quality audit management	• high complexity of audit function • high changing audit strategies/objectives • high frequency of audit risks • high audit management turnover • high level of audit performance management • high quality assurance, improvement programme • high audit process maturity • high proficiency and quality audit management

Audit Risk Mitigation

The *Beumer Audit Risk Management Model©* enables the CAE to measure and manage the internal audit risks. It must be the goal to keep the overall audit added value risk at an acceptable level. This means that the CAE needs to assess the degree of risk connected to the audit risk prevention, in order to determine the resulting risk exposures. The inherent risk and control risk influence the risk mitigation and therefore the overall audit added value risk.

Impact of audit function inherent and control risk on risk mitigation

The influence of the risk prevention on the audit risk mitigation can be described as follows:

* When the audit function inherent risk is high, and the audit function control risk is high as well, the CAE must make sure that her audit risk mitigation is high as well. In this case, the high complexity of the audit function, in combination with the function's weak control and risk management processes, cause a high likelihood that the audit function will experience significant deviations from its audit strategies and objectives. The consequence for the audit function is that there is a low level of prevention of the audit risks.

* When the audit function inherent risk is low, and the audit function control risk is low as well, the CAE can accept a low level of audit risk mitigation. The audit function has a low complexity and audit management has good control and risk management processes in place, causing a low likelihood that the audit function will experience significant deviations from its audit strategies and objectives. This means that there is a high level of prevention of the audit risks.

* When the audit function inherent risk is high, but the audit function control risk is low, the CAE must make sure that her audit risk mitigation is at a moderate level. The audit function has a high complexity but audit management has good control and risk management processes in place, causing a moderate likelihood that the audit function will experience significant deviations from its audit strategies and objectives. The CAE needs to have a good understanding of the audit function complexities to define the appropriate measures for mitigating the audit risks.

* When the audit function inherent risk is low, but the audit function control risk is high, the CAE must make sure that her audit risk

mitigation is at a moderate level. The audit function has a low complexity but audit management has weak control and risk management processes in place, causing a moderate likelihood that the audit function will experience significant deviations from its audit strategies and objectives. The CAE needs to have a good understanding of the supervision and quality control weaknesses to define the appropriate measures for mitigating the audit risks.

3ʳᵈ line of defence risk mitigation

The following model provides guidance for keeping the (residual) audit risks at an acceptable level. What constitutes an acceptable level of residual audit risk (after risk mitigation) for the audit assurance activities depends on the risk appetite of the board. The model is useful for managing and mitigating the risks relating to not achieving the target audit value (i.e. not achieving the customer's expectations or the audit function's value proposition):

Figure 11 – 3ʳᵈ Line of Defence Risk Mitigation

	Audit Function Inherent Risk is		Audit Function Control Risk is		Audit Risk Mitigation should be
	High		High		High
IF	High	AND	Low	THEN	Moderate
	Low		High		Moderate
	Low		Low		Low

PART II

-

AUDIT OBJECTIVES

Figure 12 - PART II: Audit Objectives

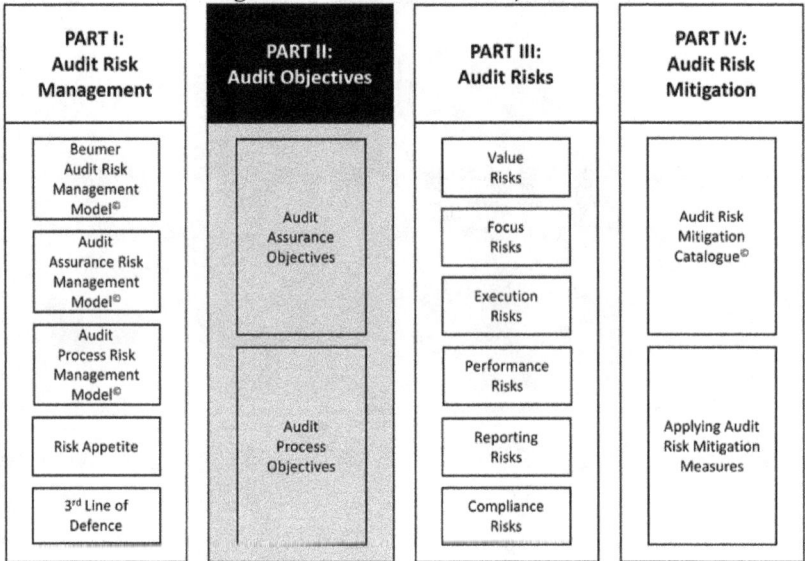

PART I: Audit Risk Management	PART II: Audit Objectives	PART III: Audit Risks	PART IV: Audit Risk Mitigation
Beumer Audit Risk Management Model©	Audit Assurance Objectives	Value Risks	Audit Risk Mitigation Catalogue©
Audit Assurance Risk Management Model©		Focus Risks	
		Execution Risks	
Audit Process Risk Management Model©	Audit Process Objectives	Performance Risks	Applying Audit Risk Mitigation Measures
Risk Appetite		Reporting Risks	
3rd Line of Defence		Compliance Risks	

Audit function objectives

Consistent with the *Beumer Audit Risk Management Model*©, the audit function's risk management starts with identifying the objectives. An audit risk is a potential event that may cause a negative deviation from the achievement of the audit function objectives. Hence, before describing the audit risks, it is necessary to determine and understand the audit objectives. The audit function objectives can be defined as:

- *Strategy Objective*: The audit strategies must be determined, aligned, communicated, implemented, and monitored.

- *Operations Objective*: The audit processes must ensure the implementation of the audit strategies through efficient and effective audit processes and use of audit resources.

- *Reporting Objective*: The audit reporting must accurately and completely reflect the audit function's activities and the achievement of the customer value proposition.

- *Compliance Objective*: The audit activities conducted by the department and the auditors must be compliant with the internal and external laws, regulations and policies.

Strategy objectives

The chapter *Audit Value* in *Driving Audit Value, Volume I*, describes the audit value in terms of the customer value proposition. Consequently, the **value objectives** are the goals for achieving the customer value proposition, by creating audit added value through:

- providing (reasonable) assurance that the company's objectives can be achieved, by generating improvements in the efficiency and effectiveness of the company's:
  - business processes
  - risk management
  - control systems

- o governance processes
- o compliance processes
- being a source of information for the board and management
- providing a talent pool and training ground for the high potential talents

The chapters *Understanding the Business and Company* and *Coordination* in *Driving Audit Value, Volume I*, describe that the right focus is obtained through the CAE's and the auditors' understanding of the business and company and the coordination of the annual audit plan and the audit engagements. *Driving Audit Value, Volume III, Audit Engagement Strategy*, builds upon the same principles for the execution of the annual audit plan. Consequently, the **focus objectives** are the goals for achieving the customer value proposition, by focusing the audit function's activities on the company's critical:

- strategies and objectives
- operations
- reporting (financial and non-financial)
- compliance

Operations objectives

The chapter *Annual Audit Plan* in *Driving Audit Value, Volume I*, describes the main product at the audit function level. *Driving Audit Value, Volume III, Audit Engagement Strategy*, describes the implementation of the annual audit plan, and the main products at the audit engagement level. Consequently, the execution objectives are the goals for achieving the customer value proposition, through a thorough execution of the:

- annual audit planning
- audit engagements
- follow-up and progress engagements

The chapters *Audit Cost* and *Performance Management* in *Driving Audit Value, Volume I*, as well as *Driving Audit Value, Volume III, Audit Engagement Strategy*, describe the four main performance management enablers. Consequently, the **performance objectives** are the goals for achieving the customer value proposition, by having an efficient and effective deployment of the audit function's:

- people
- price (cost)

- product
- process

Reporting objectives

The chapter *Reporting* in *Driving Audit Value, Volume I*, describes the seven main reporting requirements. Consequently, the **reporting objectives** are the goals for achieving the customer value proposition, through accurate and complete:

- audit committee reporting
- audit performance reporting
- annual reporting of the audit function
- annual audit plan reporting
- audit engagement reporting
- progress reporting (on the implementation of the agreed audit risk mitigation measures)
- knowledge sharing reporting

Compliance objectives

The chapter *Internal Audit Charter* in *Driving Audit Value, Volume I*, describes the five main compliance requirements. Consequently, the **compliance objectives** are the goals for achieving the customer value proposition, by ensuring compliance with the:

- audit charter
- audit policies
- company policies
- IIA's IPPF
- IIA's code of ethics

The hierarchy of the audit objectives is as follows:

Figure 13 – Audit Objectives Pyramid©

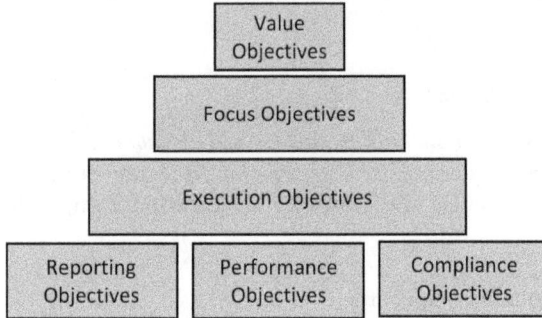

Audit Objectives Catalogue©

The *Audit Objectives Catalogue©* in Table 1 captures the 30 audit objectives in the structure of the six audit objective categories. The catalogue can be used as a checklist for identifying the audit objectives to which the audit risks can be matched.

Consistent with the *Beumer Audit Risk Management Model©*, the six audit objective categories can be split as follows:

- **Audit assurance objectives**: the audit objectives of value, focus and execution relate to the audit assurance responsibility of the audit function.

- **Audit process objectives**: The audit objectives of performance, reporting and compliance are the support processes to the audit assurance responsibility and relate to the internal processes of the audit function. In the audit risk management methodology, reporting is considered to be a communication tool for transmitting the results of the audit assurance responsibility. From this risk management's point of view, it is a support process.

Table 1 – Audit Objectives Catalogue[©]

	Audit Assurance Objectives
	1. Value Objectives
VO-1	Company business process improvements
VO-2	Company risk management improvements
VO-3	Company control systems improvements
VO-4	Company governance process improvements
VO-5	Company compliance process improvements
VO-6	Source of information for the board and management
VO-7	Talent pool and training ground
	2. Focus Objectives
FO-1	Company strategies and objectives
FO-2	Company operations
FO-3	Company reporting (financial and non-financial)
FO-4	Company compliance
	3. Execution Objectives
EO-1	Annual audit planning
EO-2	Audit engagements
EO-3	Follow-up and progress engagements
	Audit Process Objectives
	4. Performance Objectives
PO-1	Audit people
PO-2	Audit price (cost)
PO-3	Audit product
PO-4	Audit process
	5. Reporting Objectives
RO-1	Audit committee reporting
RO-2	Audit performance reporting
RO-3	Annual reporting of the audit function
RO-4	Annual audit plan reporting
RO-5	Audit engagement reporting
RO-6	Progress reporting (on the implementation of the agreed audit risk mitigation measures)
RO-7	Knowledge sharing reporting
	6. Compliance Objectives
CO-1	Audit charter
CO-2	Audit policies
CO-3	Company policies
CO-4	IIA's IPPF
CO-5	IIA's code of ethics

Audit Objectives Tree©

Figure 14 – Audit Objectives Tree©

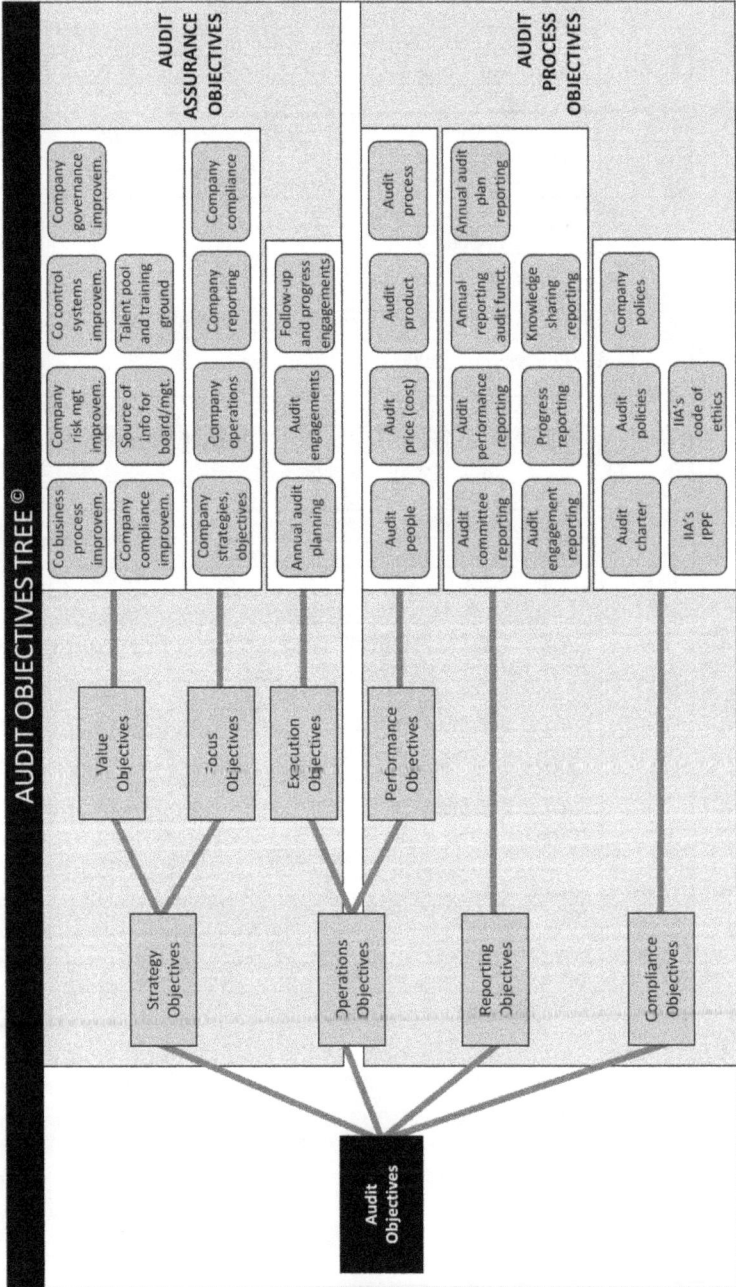

PART III
-
AUDIT
RISKS

Figure 15 - PART III: Audit Risks

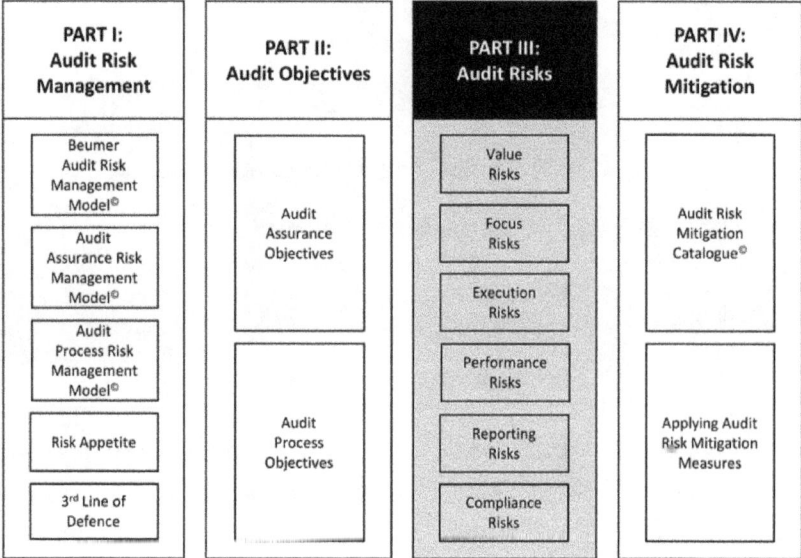

PART I: Audit Risk Management	PART II: Audit Objectives	PART III: Audit Risks	PART IV: Audit Risk Mitigation
Beumer Audit Risk Management Model©		Value Risks	
Audit Assurance Risk Management Model©	Audit Assurance Objectives	Focus Risks	Audit Risk Mitigation Catalogue©
Audit Process Risk Management Model©		Execution Risks	
		Performance Risks	
Risk Appetite	Audit Process Objectives	Reporting Risks	Applying Audit Risk Mitigation Measures
3rd Line of Defence		Compliance Risks	

Audit Risks

IPPF's audit risk definitions

Standards

The IPPF standards do not explicitly discuss the topic of audit risks and audit risk management. Of course, these could be inferred by assuming that there is an audit risk when not complying with a standard. The standards only make some general statements about audit risks in the interpretations. For example, they state that threats to the independence and objectivity must be managed. Though not specifically mentioned in *Standard 1300*, the quality assurance and improvement programme serves to ensure compliance with the standards, as well as the efficiency and effectiveness of the audit function, and thereby implicitly prevent the risk of non-added value. As such, you can say that the quality assurance should prevent the audit risks, to the extent that these relate to the audit activity processes. It is clear that non-compliance with the standards triggers certain audit process risks, which is why *Standard 1322* states that such non-conformance needs to be disclosed to senior management and the board.

Guidance

Only *Practice Advisory 2120-2 - Managing the Risk of the Internal Audit Activity*, enters into details about the risks of the audit function itself and states that the audit function must manage its risks. This non-mandatory guidance explains three risks to which an audit function can be exposed: audit failure, false assurance and reputation risk.

Audit failure

The practice advisory defines audit failure as the risk that the company incurs significant control breakdowns or fraud, which the audit function was not able to prevent. Have another look at the chapter *Where were the auditors*, which provides good examples. According to the guidance, this risk could occur when there is a non-compliance with the standards, for example due to: an inappropriate quality assurance programme; a lack of strategic risk assessments; insufficiently qualified auditors; a poor focus within the risk assessments and the work programmes; inadequate supervision; failures in the communication or the reporting.

False assurance

The practice advisory defines false assurance as the risk that management and the board believe that the audit function provided assurance on a management activity, whereas the audit function only provided resources to support that management activity, and no actual audit assurance work took place. This could occur when the auditors are "on loan", for example to support a project implementation. According to the guidance, this risk can be prevented by clear communication about the auditor's role during the support activities.

Reputation risk

The practice advisory defines reputation risk as the risk that the credibility of the audit function is severely damaged, which could occur due to one significant negative event (whereas it takes years to build up a good reputation). The listed examples for the risk mitigation are: having an effective quality assurance and improvement programme; regularly assessing the potential sources of reputation risk; and compliance with the code of ethics and with the company's policies and procedures.

Audit added value risk definition

The audit function should be run as a business. In business, the risks are defined as the potential events that may cause a negative deviation from the achievement of a certain objective. In a simplified formula, a risk has two components: a target value and an expected value. In this context, the term value can be used as a quantitative as well as a qualitative measure of the goal and the anticipated fulfilment of the goal.

Figure 16 – Generic Risk Equation

$$Risk = Expected < Target$$
$$Opportunity = Expected > Target$$

When inserting the audit added value into the equations, the simple formula looks as follows:

Figure 17 – Audit Risk Equation

$$Audit\ Risk =$$
$$Expected\ Actual\ Audit\ Added\ Value < Audit\ Added\ Value\ Objective$$

$$Audit\ Opportunity =$$
$$Expected\ Actual\ Audit\ Added\ Value > Audit\ Added\ Value\ Objective$$

This formula clearly shows that the risk component has two levers: the audit value objective and the expected actual audit value. Principally, decreasing the target audit value will reduce the risk, just as increasing the expected actual audit value will.

Decreasing the target audit value is, however, not an appropriate objective. As you can read in *Volume I* of *Driving Audit Value: Audit Function Strategy*, the objective of the audit function must be to maximise its added value. Maximising the added value of the audit function can be achieved by minimising the cost of audit, while at the same time maximising the quality and quantity of the audit value.

As analysed in *Volume I*, the target audit value is determined both by the customer expectations and the customer value proposition. In other words, an audit risk exists when not achieving the customers' expectations or when falling short on the customer value proposition. The expectations gap is the difference between the customer expectations and the customer value proposition.

Volume I also explained that the cost of audit can be optimised by performance management. So, the better the performance management, the lower the risk of having costs which are perceived to be too high in comparison to the audit value that is created.

Audit risk categories

Consistent with the *Beumer Audit Risk Management Model©*, risks need to be derived from the objectives. Following the same structure as in the chapter *Audit Function Objectives*, the following audit risks can be defined:

Strategy risks

Strategy risk: the risk that the audit function's strategic objectives are not achieved. Consistent with the strategy objectives of value and focus, two risk categories can be defined:

Value risk: the risk that the activities of the audit function do not create added value to management and the board. The annual audit plan and the audit engagements do not generate the added value required for achieving the customer value proposition. The value risk may occur in case of:

- Insufficient board and management support
- Limiting audit charter
- Poor reputation and credibility
- Expectations gap
- Outsourcing of the audit function
- Downsizing of the audit function
- Insufficient approved quantity of audit resources
- Insufficient approved quality of audit resources
- Ignoring of the audit reports by management and the board
- Rejection of the annual audit plan
- Agreed risk mitigations not being implemented by management

Focus risk: the risk that the activities of the audit function do not focus on the company's activities which are critical for management and the board to achieve their strategies and objectives. The annual audit plan does not focus on the company's main risks towards achieving their business strategies and objectives. At the audit engagement level, it is the risk that the audit engagement work does not focus on those aspects of the subject matter that may contain the main risks towards achieving the subject matter's business objectives. In other words, the annual audit plan and the audit engagements do not have the focus on the right added value topics for achieving the customer value proposition. The focus risk may occur in case of:

- Insufficient understanding of the business and company
- Insufficient risk assessments
- Insufficient access to data and information
- Insufficient coordination with the board/management
- Insufficient coordination with other assurance providers
- Narrow audit perspective
- Assurance duplications or gaps
- Insufficient auditor proficiency/experience

Operations risks

Operations risk: The risk that the audit function processes and the use of the audit resources are not effective or efficient. Consistent with the operations objectives of execution and performance, two risk categories can be defined:

Execution risk: the risk that the annual audit plan is not properly developed and implemented, or the audit engagements are not executed in a proper way, for achieving the customer value proposition. The execution risk may occur in case of:

- Insufficient auditor proficiency/experience
- Insufficient audit capacities
- Insufficient audit supervision
- Low quality work programmes
- Low quality working papers
- Scope limitations
- Insufficient coordination with the board/management
- Insufficient risk assessments
- Insufficient understanding of the business and company
- Not identifying significant issues, when they do exist
- No or wrong audit issue risk mitigation measures
- Wrong audit engagement conclusions
- Over-valuing small audit engagement issues
- Overlooking audit engagement scope limitations

Performance risk: the risk that the audit function processes and the use of the audit resources are not effective or efficient. Inefficiencies and ineffectiveness will endanger the achievement of the customer value proposition towards the board and management. The performance risk may occur in case of:

- High administrative costs
- High audit engagement costs
- High cost per audit person-day
- Low effectiveness
- Low auditor capabilities
- High auditor turnover
- Low efficiency
- Low auditor productivity
- Low auditor capacities
- Long cycle times
- Low use of technology

Reporting risks

Reporting risk*:* The risk that the audit reporting does not accurately and completely reflect the audit function's activities and the achievement of the customer value proposition. At the audit function level this can relate to reporting to executive management and the audit committee; at the audit engagement level this can relate to the audit reports. The reporting risk may occur in case of:

- Content not tailored to the recipients
- Reports not distributed to the right management
- Unclear wording and messages
- Differing format, style and layout, too many pages
- Insufficient facts and quantifications
- Subjectivity, bias and judgement
- Insufficient reporting on the audit function activities
- Audit support/consulting work perceived as audit assurance work

Compliance risks

Compliance risk: The risk that the audit activities conducted by the department and auditors are not compliant with the internal and external laws, regulations and policies. The board and management normally expect full compliance, and non-compliance will endanger the achievement of the customer value proposition. The compliance risk may occur in case of:

- Unethical behaviour
- Conflict of interest
- Subjectivity and bias in the audit activities
- Activities outside the audit function's charter
- Poor audit practices
- Travel & entertainment outside the corporate procedures
- HR management of the auditors outside the corporate procedures
- Engaging co-sourcing outside the corporate procedures

Audit Risks Catalogue©

The *Audit Risks Catalogue©* in Table 2 captures the 60 audit risks in the structure of the six audit risk categories. The catalogue can be used as a checklist for identifying the audit risks that may prevent the achievement of the audit objectives.

Table 2 – Audit Risks Catalogue©

	Audit Assurance Risks
	1. Value Risks
VR-1	Insufficient board and management support
VR-2	Limiting audit charter
VR-3	Poor reputation and credibility
VR-4	Expectations gap
VR-5	Outsourcing of audit function
VR-6	Downsizing of audit function
VR-7	Insufficient approved quantity of audit resources
VR-8	Insufficient approved quality of audit resources
VR-9	Ignoring of the audit reports by management and the board
VR-10	Rejection of the annual audit plan
VR-11	Agreed risk mitigations are not implemented by management
	2. Focus Risks
FR-1	Insufficient understanding of the business and company
FR-2	Insufficient risk assessments
FR-3	Insufficient access to data and information
FR-4	Insufficient coordination with the board/management
FR-5	Insufficient coordination with other assurance providers
FR-6	Narrow audit perspective
FR-7	Assurance duplications or gaps
FR-8	Insufficient auditor proficiency/experience
	3. Execution Risks
ER-1	Insufficient auditor proficiency/experience
ER-2	Insufficient audit capacities
ER-3	Insufficient supervision
ER-4	Low quality work programmes
ER-5	Low quality working papers
ER-6	Scope limitations
ER-7	Insufficient coordination with the board/management
ER-8	Insufficient risk assessments
ER-9	Insufficient understanding of the business and company
ER-10	Not identifying significant issues, when they do exist
ER-11	No or wrong audit issue risk mitigation measures
ER-12	Wrong audit engagement conclusions
ER-13	Over-valuing small audit engagement issues
ER-14	Overlooking audit engagement scope limitations
	Audit Process Risks
	4. Performance Risks
PR-1	High administrative costs
PR-2	High audit engagement costs
PR-3	High cost per audit person-day
PR-4	Low effectiveness
PR-5	Low auditor proficiency/experience
PR-6	High auditor turnover
PR-7	Low efficiency
PR-8	Low auditor productivity

PR-9	Low auditor capacities
PR-10	Long cycle times
PR-11	Low use of technology
5. Reporting Risks	
RR-1	Content not tailored to the recipients
RR-2	Reports not distributed to the right management
RR-3	Unclear wording and messages
RR-4	Differing format, style, layout, too many pages
RR-5	Insufficient facts and quantifications
RR-6	Subjectivity, bias and judgement
RR-7	Insufficient reporting on the audit function activities
RR-8	Audit support or consulting work being perceived as audit assurance work
6. Compliance Risks	
CR-1	Unethical behaviour
CR-2	Conflict of interest
CR-3	Subjectivity, bias and judgement
CR-4	Activities outside the audit function's charter
CR-5	Poor audit practices
CR-6	Travel & entertainment outside the corporate procedures
CR-7	HR management of the auditors outside the corporate procedures
CR-8	Engaging co-sourcing outside the corporate procedures

Interdependencies between audit risk categories

The audit assurance risk category contains 33 individual audit risks, whereas the audit process risk category contains 27 individual audit risks.

The value risks (11 out of 60) arise outside of the audit function, as it is up to the customers of the audit function to determine if the customer value proposition has been achieved. All the other risks (relating to focus, execution, performance, reporting and compliance) principally arise inside the audit function, though with certain interfaces to the customers. This means that the CAE has a direct control over 49 risks, which are under his direct responsibility. Generally, the inside risks cause the outside risks. So, when the CAE can prevent and mitigate these 49 inside risks, the 11 outside risks in the value category will not arise.

Particularly the focus risk and the value risk categories have a finer relationship of cause and effect. Value risk can be both an effect and a cause of the focus risk. In the case where management and the board do not (or insufficiently) support the audit function, it will be difficult for the CAE to ensure that the annual audit plan and the audit engagements focus on the value-added topics, and that the audit work can be executed as necessary. Insufficient support from the process owner or local management may cause certain scope limitations in the execution of the audit engagement. When the annual audit plan and the audit engagements have a poor focus and the audit work provides little added value to management and the board, the value risk is likely to increase. It is possible to receive great support from management and the board, but still incur a significant focus risk. This could be the case when the audit function does not have the best practice processes in place and does not focus on achieving the maximum added value to its customers. To the contrary, it is rather unlikely that a high focus, on the audit added value to management and the board, will lead to a significant value risk.

Audit risks overlapping between categories

Six audit risks occur in multiple audit risk categories:

- Insufficient understanding of the business and company: occurs in focus risk (FR-1) and execution risk (ER-9).
- Insufficient risk assessments: occurs in focus risk (FR-2) and execution risk (ER-8).
- Insufficient coordination with the board/management: occurs in focus risk (FR-4) and execution risk (ER-7).
- Insufficient auditor proficiency/experience: occurs in focus risk (FR-8), execution risk (ER-1) and performance risk (PR-5).

- Insufficient audit capacities: occurs in execution risk (ER-2) and performance risk (PR-9).
- Subjectivity, bias and judgement: occurs in reporting risk (RR-6) and compliance risk (CR-3).

This means that with a single risk mitigating action, audit risks in multiple risk categories can be addressed. When these double counts are eliminated, the net number of audit risks amounts to 53.

Audit Risks Portfolio©

The *Audit Risks Portfolio©* captures these 60 most common audit risks in one risk map. Use the following guidance for the interpretation of this model:

- The risks are measured as the potential impact and likelihood of a deviation from achieving the targeted audit added value, the customer value proposition, or the targeted audit strategies and audit objectives.

- In order to make the large number of 60 individual risks manageable, they have been clustered into the six main categories: value risks, focus risks, execution risks, reporting risks, performance risks, and compliance risks.

- The positions of the (clustered) risks are based on two criteria: the absolute and the relative impact and likelihood. The absolute criteria determine the position based on the expected deviations from the audit objectives, whereas the relative criteria determine the position based on the comparison between the six risk categories.

- The value risks are customer related risks. The reporting risks are risks in the direct interfaces between the audit function and the customers. The focus risks are partially in the interfaces with the customers and partially audit function internal processes. The compliance risks are partially in the interfaces with others and partially audit function internal processes. The execution risks are mostly audit function internal processes, with a small interface to the customers. The performance risks are fully audit function internal processes.

Figure 18 – Audit Risks Portfolio©

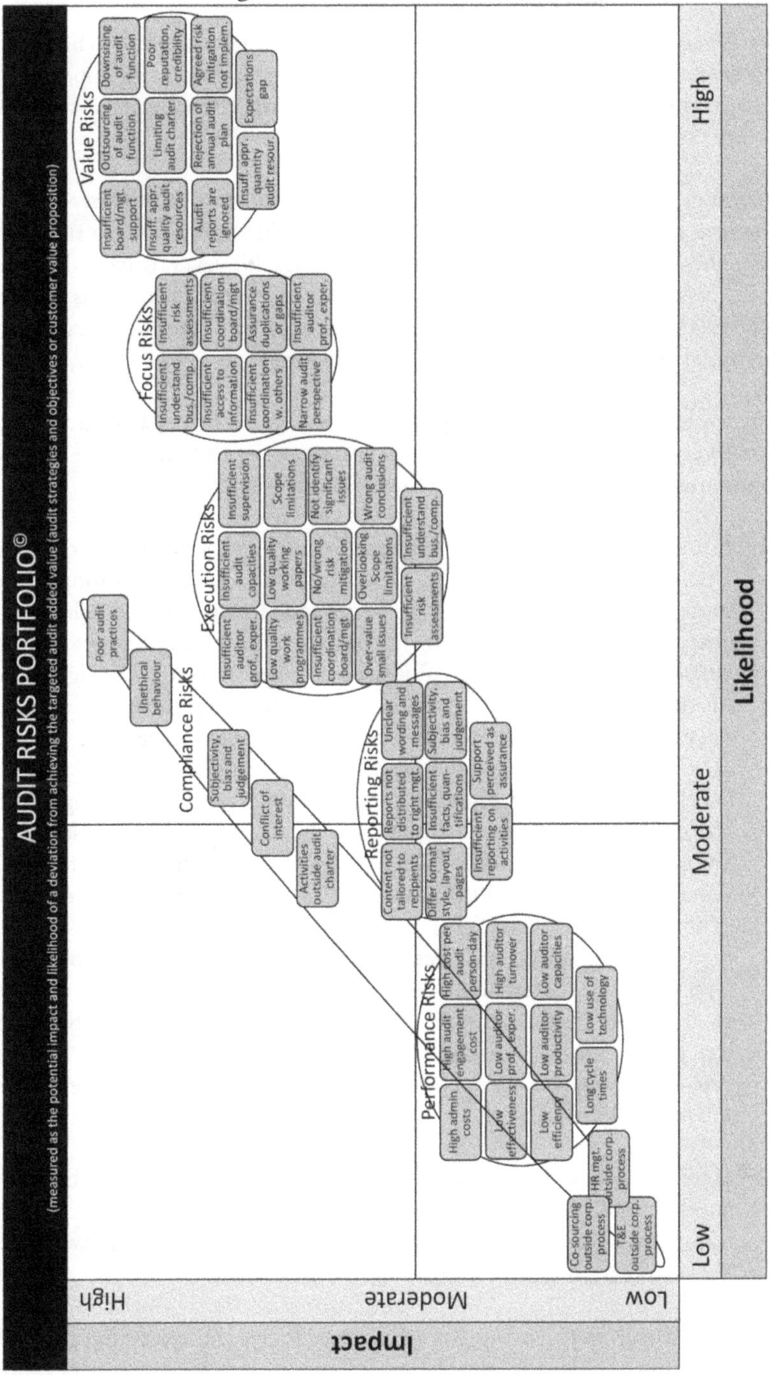

Priorities among audit risk categories

The *Audit Risks Portfolio*© shows the generic risk landscape to which each and every audit function is exposed. The audit objectives, risk appetite and the risk prevention for a particular audit function will determine which of the risks may occur, as well as their exact impact and likelihood.

According to the *Audit Risk Portfolio*© the CAE should have the overarching objective to prevent and mitigate the outside value risks, as these risks rank the highest in the risk map. These value risks are, however, usually the result of the risks occurring in the other five risk categories. This means that the value risks can be reduced by mitigation of the risks in the focus, execution, performance, reporting and compliance categories.

When a new CAE assumes responsibility for an audit department, he will have to concentrate his efforts and set priorities. In such cases, the order of importance of managing the audit function's risks are:

1st **Focus risk**: only a focus on the board, management and company strategies, objectives and the resulting risk profile (company risk universe), has the power to generate added value and to achieve the customer value proposition. These risks have the highest impact, which is why they must be addressed as a first priority. The right focus of the audit function's activities is on the main business and risk concerns of the board and executive management. They will care less about the efficiency of the audit function, the way the audit function executes the audit engagements, whether the audit function signed the IIA's code of ethics, or whether the audit function uses audit automation software. The board's biggest expectation is of the audit function's capability to provide a substantial audit assurance coverage of the company's risk universe. Achieve that, and the board will have a high level of satisfaction, despite everything else that goes on in the audit function's internal processes. The importance in focus is reflected in the size of the annual audit planning process. It is the audit function's most time-consuming, intensive, critical and difficult process. My personal experience is that when you get this focus right, the rest will follow.

2nd **Execution risk**: the audit function may have the right focus, but if the annual audit plan and the audit engagements are not executed in the right way, value may still not be achieved. As execution follows focus, these risks must be addressed as a second priority.

3rd **Reporting risk**: having the right audit focus and executing the audit work in the right way may be meaningless when the customers cannot understand the reports and messages. Then the added value of the audit activities does not get transmitted to them. As reporting follows execution, these risks must be addressed as a third priority.

4th **Compliance risk:** compliance risks should be relatively easy to resolve and mitigate, through short-term efforts. Reducing compliance risks will put the audit function in line with the basic requirements derived from the audit function charter and policies, company policies and the IIA's IPPF and code of ethics.

The compliance risks relating to good audit practices and ethical behaviour may have a high impact on the value creation. These risks should actually be mitigated with a higher priority, probably even as a first priority. Having the right focus entails applying a good audit practice. The board has the expectation that the audit value is created through processes compliant with the company's code of conduct. They will have the implicit, unspoken, expectation that the auditors conduct their activities in an ethical way. Any breach in ethics may seriously endanger the value-add, even when the audit function has the right focus, has a good execution and is extremely efficient and effective. Compared to the focus risk, however, the likelihood of the compliance risk will be much lower. In my personal experience, auditors always behave very ethical, however, they do not always have the right focus (which brings the focus risk back to the number one priority).

5th **Performance risk:** the efficiency and effectiveness of the audit function may optimise the methods with which the added value is delivered. Since these are internal processes, fully under the control of the CAE, it is often tempting to give their improvement a priority over the mitigation of the focus and execution risks. Risk mitigations for the internal processes may be easy and fast to achieve, however, their contribution to creating added value to the board is minimal in comparison to the focus and execution objectives.

Prioritisation of the topics in Part II, III and IV of this book

These priorities for managing the audit function's risks show the way that the content of this book should be interpreted. When reading through the six categories of the audit objectives, audit risks and audit risk mitigations, bear in mind this overarching order of priority and importance.

Audit Assurance Risks

Figure 19 – Three Audit Assurance Risk Categories

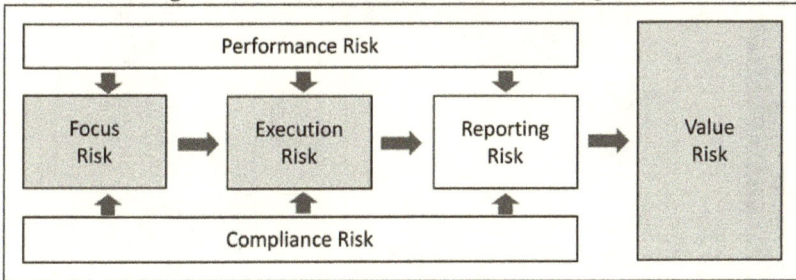

In the next three chapters, each of the three audit assurance risk categories, together with the 33 risks from the *Audit Risks Catalogue©*, are described and analysed in detail. The chapters have the following structure:

- A risk matrix matches the risks from the audit risks catalogue with the audit function objectives from the *Audit Objectives Catalogue©*.

- A risk map matches the risks from the audit risks catalogue with the achievement of the customer value proposition.

- The key conclusions from the risk matrix and risk map single out the topics for analysis and explanation. The selected topics are detailed in:
  - o defining the risk, followed by examples and an analysis of the causes;
  - o describing the impact of the risks on the audit function itself, as well as the impact from the perspective of the process owner, division/business unit management, executive management and the audit committee/board;
  - o analysing the risk drivers, as well as guidance for assessing the level of the risk.

Audit Assurance Risk Tree©

Figure 20 – Audit Assurance Risk Tree©

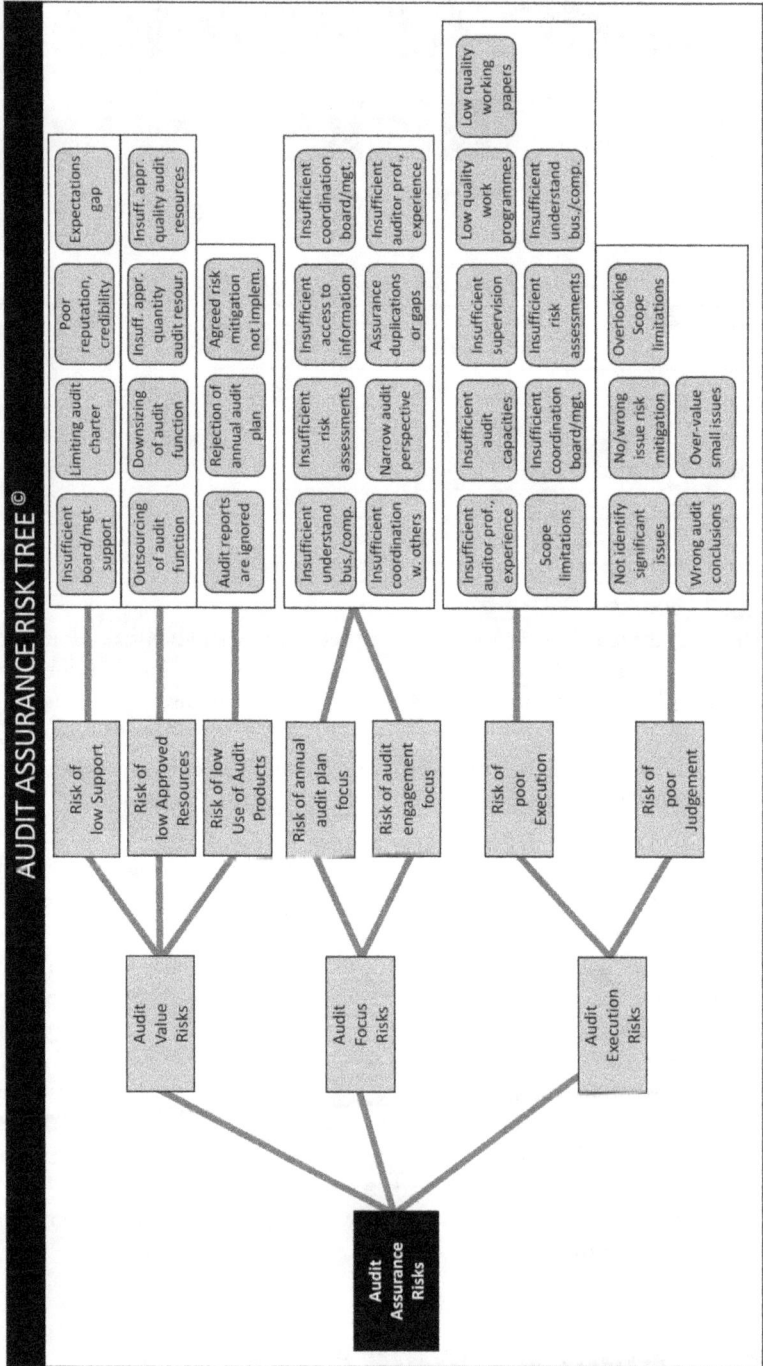

Audit Risk 1: Value Risks

Figure 21 – Eleven Elements of Value Risk

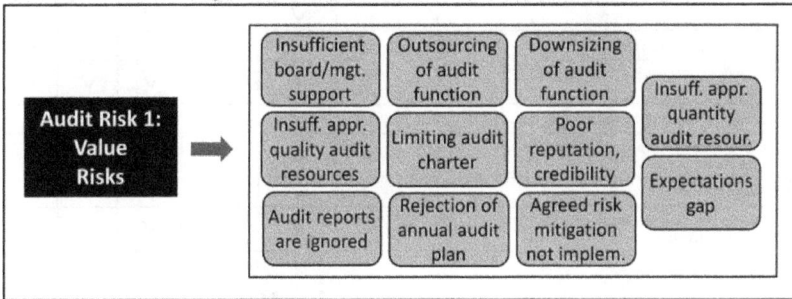

The value risk is the risk that the activities of the audit function do not create added value to management and the board. The annual audit plan and the audit engagements do not generate the added value required for achieving the customer value proposition.

In the following Value Risk Matrix, the 11 value risks from the *Audit Risks Catalogue*© are matched with the seven value objectives from the *Audit Objectives Catalogue*©. In the Value Risk Map, the 11 value risks are mapped to the audit function's customer value proposition. The conclusions from this matrix and map are:

- All 11 risks apply to the five main value objectives for improving the company to help it reach its objectives.

- The risks can be clustered in three main categories: risks of support, risks of approved resources and risks of acceptance of the audit products.

- All the risks have a substantial negative impact on the achievement of the customer value proposition.

Figure 22 – Value Risk Matrix

Value Risks: \ Value Objectives:	VO-1: Company business improvements	VO-2: Company risk management improvements	VO-3: Company control systems improvements	VO-4: Company governance processes improvements	VO-5: Company compliance processes improvements	VO-6: Source of information for the board and management	VO-7: Talent pool and training ground
VR-1: Insufficient board and management support	✓	✓	✓	✓	✓	✓	✓
VR-2: Limiting audit charter	✓	✓	✓	✓	✓	✓	✓
VR-3: Poor reputation and credibility	✓	✓	✓	✓	✓	✓	✓
VR-4: Expectations gap	✓	✓	✓	✓	✓	✓	✓
VR-5: Outsourcing of audit function	✓	✓	✓	✓	✓	✓	✓
VR-6: Downsizing of audit function	✓	✓	✓	✓	✓	✓	✓
VR-7: Insufficient approved quantity of audit resources	✓	✓	✓	✓	✓	✓	✓
VR-8: Insufficient approved quality of audit resources	✓	✓	✓	✓	✓	✓	✓
VR-9: Ignoring of audit reports by management and the board	✓	✓	✓	✓	✓	✓	
VR-10: Rejection of the annual audit plan	✓	✓	✓	✓	✓		
VR-11: Agreed risk mitigations are not implemented by management	✓	✓	✓	✓	✓		

Figure 23 – Value Risk Map

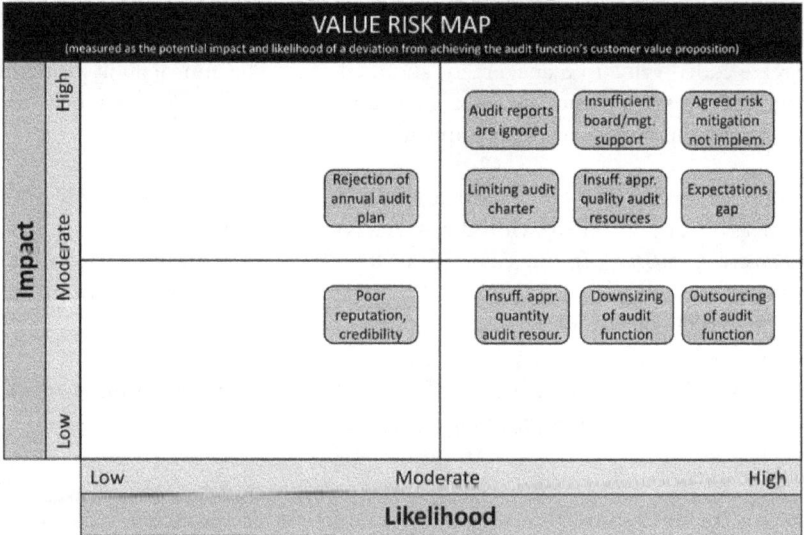

VALUE RISK MAP
(measured as the potential impact and likelihood of a deviation from achieving the audit function's customer value proposition)

The chapter is divided into three sections:

1. Risk of low support (VR-1 to 4)
2. Risk of low approved resources (VR-5 to 8)
3. Risk of low use of the audit products (VR-9 to 11)

Risk of low support

Definition

Support risk is the risk that the audit function receives insufficient support, as a result of which the annual audit plan, or the audit engagement, does not focus on the company's main risks towards achieving its strategies and objectives. In such a case, the audit function receives little support from the process owner, management or the board, and they do not take the results of the audit work seriously. Access to the process owner, key management or the board may be limited, as they do not make the time available for discussions with the CAE or the audit team.

Examples

Management does not provide the information needed for the understanding of the emerging risk profile and business developments. The higher management levels may show no interest in discussing the annual audit plan priorities or the audit engagement results. Perhaps the CAE is never invited to the periodic global management meetings, as executive management does not consider her part of the corporate team. The audit charter limits the mandate of the audit function to low level control and system reviews.

Causes

The causes of the support risk can both lie within and outside the audit function. It has an internal cause when: the audit function has a low credibility or a bad reputation; the CAE insufficiently markets and promotes her internal audit services; she is not able to "connect" with management; the audit results never catch the interest of management. The audit reports could either have no interesting issues, or the quality of the reports could be very low (for example, due to poor English, irrelevant data being presented, wrong conclusions, or chaotic presentation of the topics).

The support risk may have an external cause when the management capacity is too thin, or when management is fire-fighting big problems in their business (and audit work is simply not a priority). Problems of support by the individual managers may be caused by a disinterest, a bad personal experience with the audit function, or a person may have something to hide. The support risk can also be caused by an expectations gap, when the board and management expect much more than the audit function/CAE can deliver.

Impact on audit function

Receiving limited or no support makes it hard to generate added value to the process owner, management and the board. Even when the audit function does a good job, they will not care and will not reward it.

Impact on process owner

The process owner or local management is usually not involved in the selection of topics for the annual audit plan, hence at that level, their non-support does not play a role.

Their non-support, however, does play a significant role at the level of the audit engagement. When the audit function receives no support from the auditee, process owner or local management, it is extremely difficult to execute the audit work. The audit work may then be limited to document reviews, and in a worst-case scenario, the process owner does not support the interviews. Audit work can be performed on the core systems for which the paper documentation trials of the transactions exist. When reviewing topics that need intensive discussions (such as the topics with a high complexity or a high judgemental content), the audit function incurs a serious scope limitation.

Impact on division/business unit management

By discussing the relevant topics for the audit planning and the audit engagement execution with the higher levels of management or the corporate functions, the audit function can compensate for a lack of division/business unit management's support. At the corporate level, the CAE might be able to obtain the relevant documents for assessing the completeness of the audit universe, business developments, and so forth. Still, if the division/business unit managers do not support the work, they could work against the audit function, block the audit of the selected engagements, comment negatively on the audit results or on the way that the audit function provides its services. They could have a strong negative influence on the higher-level managers such as the CEO.

Impact on executive management

If executive management does not support the audit function, it gets complicated. They set the tone for the behaviour and when they do not take the audit function seriously, neither will the lower-level managers. This will cause a serious problem for achieving the customer value proposition. In case the non-support results in executive management ignoring the CAE, then she still has some chances of creating the added value in cooperation with the other corporate functions and the lower levels of management. But for that to work, the CAE needs to have good personal relationships with those other managers. I had the personal experience of such a case, and indeed, it was still possible, with the support of the audit committee and the other levels of management, to generate the added value. In case the non-support results in executive management blocking the CAE, it becomes very difficult to achieve the customer value proposition.

Impact on audit committee/board

The stance of the (chairman of the) audit committee may also vary between limited to full support. When the CAE has no support from the board, but full support from executive management, she is still able to generate the full added value, after all, most of the time she deals with management. When both the board and executive management do not give support, the CAE may try to change this; but if she is not successful, then she is in the wrong governance environment.

Risk drivers

The following risk drivers have a significant influence on the level of the support risk, and the lower each of these elements, the higher the risk:

- The level of credibility and reputation of the audit function.
- The way the CAE "connects" with the process owner, management and the board, the way the CAE speaks their language, and the quality of their relationships.
- The goal-congruence between the focus of the audit function and the focus of the process owner, management and the board. The bigger the expectations gap, the greater the support risk.
- Management's and the board's view on the principles of good governance and the added value role of the audit function.
- The quality of management, or how quickly their job becomes too much, regarding the handling of their daily business challenges.

Determining risk levels

The audit function has a high support risk when: management does not want, or has no time, to be involved in the audit function and the audit work; the CAE is not given access to critical business information; she is not invited to the periodic global management meetings; the proposed audit plans are frequently rejected; management wants the audit function to focus on the low-level control systems only; the CAE never meets the CEO to discuss the audit topics and priorities; the CAE needs to show the audit charter to get management cooperating; the audit reports are not read or taken seriously; the process owner blocks access to important parts of the subject matter.

The audit function has a low support risk when: management is always open for discussion; they provide all the information requested; they approach the CAE with requests for audit work; the CAE gets invited to the periodic leadership meetings; they show interest in the significant audit findings; they provide high-quality input into the annual audit planning and the engagement scoping; the process owner provides full transparency and disclosure on the important aspects of the subject matter.

Risk of low approved resources

Definition

The risk of low approved resources is the risk that the board and executive management limit the quantity and quality of the audit resources by limiting the approved headcount/FTE and financial budget (for reasons other than adjusting the size of the audit function to the company's business and cyclical developments). This is a risk of under-sizing of the audit function.

Examples

The company has more than 200 operational entities and over 100'000 employees, however, the board and executive management set the budget for the audit function at such a level that only 15 audit FTEs can be employed. This results in a number of audit employees and an audit budget far below the industry average ratios for the number of audit employees per 1'000 company employees and the audit budget as percentage of the company turnover.

I refer to *Driving Audit Value, Volume I: Audit Function Strategy*, chapter *Audit Cost* for a detailed analysis on the topic of right-sizing of the audit function.

Causes

The cause of this risk can lie within the audit function, or outside the audit function. It has an internal cause when the audit function was never able to generate added value or when the CAE was never able to close a significant expectations gap. This can convince the board and management of the diminished value of the audit function, as a result of which they decided to cut the costs and resources of the audit function. This could even go as far as deciding it not being worthwhile in having an in-house audit function (for quality, value, cost or flexibility reasons) and thus to completely outsource the audit activity.

The risk may have an external cause when management is a strong believer of outsourcing based on expected quality and cost flexibility or is generally not convinced of the role and benefit of an (in-house) audit function.

Impact on audit function

The result of not achieving the customer value proposition is that executive management and the board may consider the perceived value of the audit function below their expectations. They might give the CAE the assignment to increase the value of the audit function, or they might think that the CAE is the wrong person for the job. They might have considerations to outsource the audit function, to replace the CAE with a new leader or to downsize the audit function. Therefore, for the success of the audit function, as well as for the CAE's career, she needs to mitigate this value risk with priority.

A reduced audit function budget may have two impacts: a lower quantity of the audit headcounts and/or a lower quality of the audit headcounts. It can be argued that with a lower quantity of headcounts (but still of good quality), the CAE should still be able to achieve the audit function's value proposition. This can be achieved by sharpening the focus in the annual audit plan. It means doing fewer audits, but still focus the remaining audits on the highly added value topics. Instead of covering the top 30 company risks, the CAE might still be able to cover the top 20 business risks. Conversely, lowering the quality of the headcounts may increase the value risk. The CAE might not be able to cover any of the top business risks anymore, because the auditors are too inexperienced to perform audit work on complex and judgemental topics.

Impact on process owner

The auditee, process owner or local management, are impacted by a limitation of the audit resources in two ways. Firstly, they may be visited for audit with a lower frequency, or with a lower duration. Generally speaking, local management will be quite content with fewer visits from the audit team. In case the quality of the auditors was lowered, they may have to spend more time in explanations and discussions during the audit field work.

Impact on division/business unit management

The impact on division/business unit management is the same. They will receive a lower audit coverage of the risks in their businesses. Generally speaking, division/business unit management will be content with fewer visits from the audit team, though some of these business leaders may find it a pity that they receive less assurance on the quality of their risk management and internal control systems. In case the quality of the audit auditors was lowered, they may have to spend more time in explanations and discussions, and they may receive less interesting audit findings.

Impact on executive management and audit committee/board

It will be executive management, in coordination with the board, who have decided to lower the resources of the audit function. This means that they accept a lower audit assurance coverage, as they probably considered the assurances in the past to be below their expectations.

Risk drivers

The following risk drivers have a major influence on the level of the resources risk, and the lower each of these elements, the higher the risk:

- The level of significance of the audit issues, and linked to that, the right focus of the annual audit plan.
- The number and quality of audit reports produced.
- The level of leverage of the audit cost.
- The level of the productivity, efficiency and effectiveness of the audit function.

Determining risk levels

The audit function has a high resources risk when: it never raises any significant audit issues; the annual audit plan only covers low-risk areas; productivity of the auditors is low; each auditor produces very few audit reports in a year; the average cost per audit day is higher than the comparable costs of outsourcing.

The audit function has a low resources risk when: management is strongly supporting the audit function; all audit reports are taken seriously, and the audit results are frequently discussed in the executive management meetings and the audit committee; the annual audit plan focuses on the high-risk areas of the company; the CAE is actively managing productivity and performance; productivity is high; the average cost per audit day is far below the comparable costs of outsourcing.

Risk of low use of the audit products

Definition

Low use of the audit products is the risk that the board and management do not perceive the annual audit plan, audit engagement reports or the audit issue risk mitigating measures to be of added value. In such a case, they think that they are getting too little, or too low quality, value from the audit function and they do not take the audit function's work products seriously.

Examples

The board and executive management frequently reject the proposed annual audit plan, wanting that the CAE focuses the audit assurance on lower level risks and control systems. The audit reports are hardly ever read by management, and the CAE never receives any questions from the recipients of the reports. The audit issue risk mitigations agreed with local management, and documented in the audit reports, are hardly implemented. Local management decides to implement what they think is the right risk mitigation or they do not implement risk reductions at all.

Causes

The cause of this value risk can lie within the audit function, or outside the audit function. It has an internal cause when the internal audit reports are not clear enough (for example, due to the poor English, irrelevant data being presented, the wrong conclusions, or the chaotic presentation of the topics), when the annual audit plan does not have the right focus, or when the audit engagement's results never capture the interest of the process owner, management or the board.

This value risk may have an external cause when management is not convinced of the role and benefit of an audit function.

Impact on audit function

It will be very demotivating for the CAE and the audit team when they work hard to generate their products, but management and the board do not appreciate or recognise the value of the work results. In case the audit function does its work only half-heartedly and is aware that they produce mediocre quality work results, the rejections by the board and management must be a clear signal that they need to enhance the quality of the focus and results of their audit assurance. It may also be a signal that they need to improve the method of delivery with the reports as the carrying vehicle of their messages. A low use of the work results must trigger a quality improvement process.

Impact on process owner

When the auditee, process owner or local management, perceives the value of the audit work to be low, it means that they are not directly benefitting from the audit review. That could happen when the audit function is reviewing processes for which the process owner believes there is no benefit in evaluating these, as the risks lie somewhere else. Most of the time, the process owner will succumb to the audit work, and will not complain about it. After all, if the audit function is reviewing a work area that has good internal controls, he does not expect any significant issues to be raised. He expects a clean report, which will make him look good towards higher management and the board. So, the process owner has a "win" when the audit work does not add value, and he does not need to give it much management attention. He will have the positive thought that he received a clean report, but with a cynical view that the audit was useless. However, if the audit function wants to do an audit like that, who is the process owner to object.

Impact on division/business unit management

In case division/business unit management perceives the value of the audit work as too low, they might not tell the CAE directly, but complain to the CEO instead. They will express their view that their organisation needs to make significant time available for enabling the audit work, but that they receive poor quality audit results, poorly formulated audit reports, and do not see any benefit of the audit work. They will complain behind the CAE's back and expect the CEO to talk to the CAE about improving the value of the audit work.

Impact on executive management

If executive management perceives the results of the audit work to be of low value, they might let it go for a while. Depending on how busy they are with their business topics, eventually, they will address it with the CAE. If they are good managers they will bring up the issue as soon as it arises, alternatively, they may wait till the CAE's annual performance review. In case of the latter, it will be too late for the CAE to take corrective actions to safeguard her bonus achievement, and she may lose quite a bit of money. It depends on how long they let it go before they address the topic with her. The longer they wait, the higher the risk that they may take stringent actions (such as replacing the CAE, outsourcing or downsizing the audit function), having come to the conclusion that the CAE is the wrong person for the job. If they tell her early, they believe that she has the capability to turn the situation around. When the CEO and CFO believe that the audit function is not adding value, they may also develop an indifference to the audit work. They could think that they have no choice but to accept an audit function from the board's governance perspective, and they might just push the CAE, the audit function and the audit work results aside, as necessary but harmless. When they do not urge the CAE to improve the added value, who else will?

Impact on audit committee/board

If the (chairman of the) audit committee believes that the audit function does not deliver the added value, they might ask the CAE some probing questions to get a better view of what is causing the problem. If they do not get a good view of the problem or the root causes, they will enter into a discussion with executive management. They will ask the CEO or CFO to sort it out and come up with a proposal to improve the situation. As explained before, this proposal could entail giving the CAE another chance, replacing her, downsizing or outsourcing the audit function. It is all up to the CAE to prevent this from happening by mitigating the value risk.

Risk drivers

The following risk drivers have a major influence on the level of this value risk, and the lower each of these elements, the higher the risk:

- The right focus of the annual audit plan on those business topics which are of concern to management and the board.
- The level of significance of the audit issues.
- The cost-effectiveness and efficiency of the suggested audit risk mitigation measures.
- The quality of the audit reports.

Determining risk levels

The audit function has a high value risk when: it never raises any significant audit issues; the annual audit plan only covers low-risk areas; the recommendations for the issue risk mitigations are inefficient and too expensive; the audit reports are more than 120 pages; the audit reports have unclear wording and messages, and poor English.

The audit function has a low value risk when: the audit results are frequently discussed in the executive management meetings and the audit committee; the annual audit plan focuses on the high-risk areas of the company; the recommended audit issue risk mitigating measures are efficient, effective and have a low cost of implementation and maintenance; the audit reports are short and concise, with clear wording and messages.

Audit Risk 2: Focus Risks

Figure 24 – Eight Elements of Focus Risk

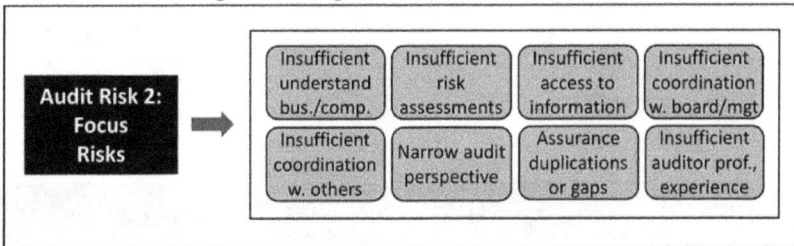

The focus risk is the risk that the activities of the audit function do not focus on the company's activities which are critical for management and the board to achieve their strategies and objectives. The annual audit plan does not focus on the company's main risks towards achieving their business strategies and objectives. At the audit engagement level, it is the risk that the audit engagement work does not focus on those aspects of the subject matter that may have the main risks towards achieving the subject matter's business objectives.

In the following Focus Risk Matrix, the eight focus risks from the *Audit Risks Catalogue*© are matched with the four focus objectives from the *Audit Objectives Catalogue*©. In the Focus Risk Map, the eight focus risks are mapped to the audit function's customer value proposition. The conclusions from this matrix and map are:

All the eight risks apply to all the four objectives. This means that all these focus risks can occur in the annual audit planning as well as in the individual audit engagements.

- The focus risks are based on six equally critical elements: the level of understanding the business/subject matter, assessing the company/subject matter risks, coordination, proficiency and experience of the auditors, access to information and the width of the audit perspective.

Figure 25 – Focus Risk Matrix

FOCUS RISK MATRIX				
Focus Risks: / Focus Objectives:	FO-1: Company strategies and objectives	FO-2: Company operations	FO-3: Company reporting	FO-4: Company compliance
FR-1: Insufficient understanding of the business and company	✓	✓	✓	✓
FR-2: Insufficient risk assessments	✓	✓	✓	✓
FR-3: Insufficient access to data and information	✓	✓	✓	✓
FR-4: Insufficient coordination with the board/management	✓	✓	✓	✓
FR-5: Insufficient coordination with other assurance providers	✓	✓	✓	✓
FR-6: Narrow audit perspective	✓	✓	✓	✓
FR-7: Assurance duplications or gaps	✓	✓	✓	✓
FR-8: Insufficient auditor proficiency / experience	✓	✓	✓	✓

Figure 26 – Focus Risk Map

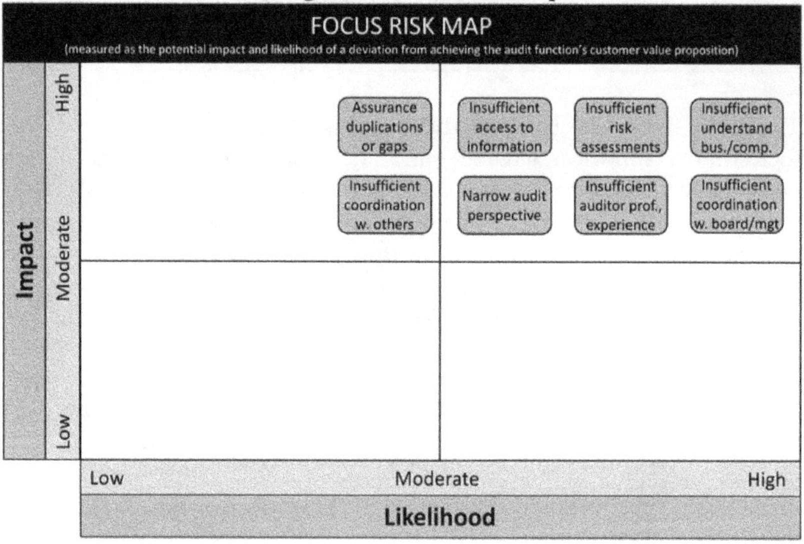

FOCUS RISK MAP
(measured as the potential impact and likelihood of a deviation from achieving the audit function's customer value proposition)

The focus risks principally relate to the two main aspects of the audit activity: the annual audit plan and the audit engagements. Since all the eight risks apply to all the four objectives as well as the two main activities, these risks can be commonly described under the caption of focus risk in the remainder of this chapter.

Definition

Focus risk is the risk that the annual audit plan does not focus on the company's main risks towards achieving its strategy objectives, its operations objectives, its reporting objectives and its compliance objectives.

In such a case, the selection of the audit topics fails to address the significant risks and objectives of the company. Instead, audit assurance is provided over topics that provide little added value to management and the board, as the annual audit plan focuses on the "wrong" topics.

At the audit engagement level this risk is the same: the audit engagement work does not focus on those aspects of the subject matter that may contain the main risks towards achieving the subject matter objectives.

Examples

The annual audit plan includes audits relating to the internal controls in the sales processes of three large entities. Previous internal audits never raised any red flag issues (it is a low risk), but these audits are selected based on the rotation principle. However, the CAE fails to identify that one of the entities has extensive product recall campaigns, another one is falling significantly short on its objective to reduce the time-to-market for the new product developments, and the third entity will be divested as part of a strategic initiative to focus on the core business. As a result, the audits provide assurance over the standard internal controls within the sales processes, whereas the primary risk exposures respectively lie in the product quality management system, the research and development process, and the divestment process.

The annual audit plan includes a topic relating to the purchasing processes. The plan is to execute several audits providing assurance on the basic internal controls in the purchasing processes of three business units. However, the CAE failed to identify that these purchasing processes were going to be completely reorganised six months later. Or he neglected to identify that management has launched a major strategic initiative to reduce the cost of purchased materials by 40 percent. As a result, the audits provide assurance on the basic internal controls within the purchasing processes, whereas the primary risk exposures lie in the upcoming reorganisation or the realisation of the significant cost reductions.

Causes

The cause of the focus risk can lie within the audit function, or outside the audit function. It has an internal cause when the annual audit planning process does not pick up on the emerging risks, when asking the wrong questions or having incomplete sources of information. This could be caused by a weak risk assessment process, an incomplete audit universe, or not understanding the business well enough. The focus risk may have an external cause when management intentionally withholds critical information on emerging risks, when management thinks that such information is not essential for the audit plans, because they do not sufficiently understand the focus of the audit work, or when management considers the information beyond the remit of the audit function. The same applies for the subject matter of the audit engagements.

Impact on audit function

The result of having a wrong focus in the annual audit plan is that the audit assurance will be provided over topics that are low on the priority list of executive management and the board. This means that they are going to perceive the added value of the audit function to be mediocre or low. This is not good for the reputation and credibility of the CAE, or for the whole audit function. At the audit engagement level, the lack of focus may result in the audit work not being conducted on the high-risk processes of the subject matter. The focus risk has a direct impact on the value risk.

Impact on process owner

The auditee, process owner or local management, generally will not care that they are being audited, instead of another entity, another process or another project (that should have been chosen with a higher priority). They do not have the overview of what is necessary for the selection in the annual audit plan. Usually, they accept being selected for an audit, without arguing that the risks in another part of the company, or in another part of their entity, are higher, and thus the audit function should visit them instead. In case they are aware of the higher risks in other parts of their entity, or other areas of the company, they might wonder why they, and not the others, were selected for an audit. Similarly, when the audit engagement focuses on parts of the subject matter that have a low relevance to achieve the process owner's objectives. They might discuss this internally while gossiping in the canteen or around the coffee machine, but they seldom bring this up for discussion with the audit function. Though they might not express themselves to the audit function, it could cause an undercurrent of doubts about the focus of the audit function, and thereby reduce the reputation and credibility.

Impact on division/business unit management

Division/business unit management's reaction could go either way. A value driven business unit leader will question the selection of the projects, as she will want to extract the maximum value from the audit work. She will want a focus on the right topics and expects support in identifying and addressing those risks that make her lie awake at night. To the contrary, a business unit leader who wants to make sure that he receives audit reports without significant issues, will probably keep his mouth shut. He might think that the audit function should concentrate on some basic process controls, whereas he will continue to address and manage the significant risks in his business. He might even think that it should not be within the mandate of the audit function to review the important business issues.

Impact on executive management

Executive management expects the audit function to provide added value by focusing on the right topics. However, what is the "right" topic may differ a bit in their eyes. For example, I have the experience with a CEO who wanted our audit function to concentrate on the (low-level) compliance processes and risks within the company. He considered the topics relating to the strategy implementation his responsibility. I also have the experience with a CEO who did not care at all and a CEO who cared very much that we were addressing the topics of importance to the company as a whole. It is as described for the business unit head; with the CEO, it could also go either way. From the perspective of executive management, the focus risk could either not exist (because they want the audit function to focus on the low-level internal control topics and avoid the business topics) or could exist.

Impact on audit committee/board

The audit committee will not get involved in the details of the selection of the audit projects in the annual audit plan. Usually they accept what is presented to them, unless executive management has expressed disagreement with the plan, or unless the plan is significantly misjudging the risk profile of the company. This means that when the annual plan focuses on rather low-level risks or does not address the primary business objectives, the board might not object. The board will therefore not necessarily prevent the focus risks, at the time that the CAE is putting together or presenting the annual audit plan. The CAE needs to understand the board's focus, and from there derive his conclusions of what can be of importance to the audit plan. When the board approves a low-risk focus audit plan, they will not bring-up the question of a wrong focus once the CAE starts executing the plan. After all, they approved it, and the CAE is expected to implement the approved plan. Although they will not bring it up to the CAE, they will think that the added value of the audit function is limited, when the plan does not address the big-ticket items that are on their mind. They might believe that the audit function is suitable in providing the assurance on the core internal controls, risk management and governance processes, but that the audit function has no qualification to address the significant business issues. This means that they will either talk negatively about the audit function, or more likely is actually, that they will not speak of the audit function at all among themselves. This means that it is up to the CAE to bring the added value focus to the table of the audit committee/board. This is why the coordination aspect is so important. I refer to the chapter *Coordination* in *Volume I* of *Driving Audit Value*.

Risk drivers

The following risk drivers have a significant influence on the level of the focus risk, and the lower each of these elements, the higher the risk:

- The level of understanding of the business, company and subject matter.
- The quality of the analysis of the risks and the business objectives.
- The level of input by and coordination with the process owner, management and the board, as well as with the other assurance providers.
- The completeness of the audit universe, access to information.
- The auditor's proficiency and experience with annual audit planning and audit engagement planning.

The focus risk may also be caused by management not providing the information needed to make a full audit plan or audit engagement assessment. A theoretical possibility is of course also, that the information is received, but that the CAE does not (or is not able to) assess its importance.

Determining risk levels

The annual audit plan process or the audit engagement has a high focus risk when: the business is highly complex; working for a conglomerate with a multitude of different businesses; there are frequent and significant changes to the business; management does not want, or has no time, to be involved in the selection process; management has an outdated perception of the role of the audit function; the CAE is not able to think like a business person (narrow audit perspective); the CAE has no access to key business managers and information; the CAE does not coordinate the focus with management, the board and the other assurance providers.

The annual audit plan process or the audit engagement has a low focus risk when: the business and business models are easy to understand; the business and their processes are mature with few changes; management is very responsive to the planning requirements and makes the time available for support; the CAE has all the business-related documents he needs for completing the audit universe and the engagement scoping; the process owner, board and management want the audit function to focus on the important business topics; the auditors are proficient and experienced.

A word of caution

The above explanations all refer to the risk of not having the right focus within the annual audit plan or the audit engagement. Perhaps a word of caution at this point; I refer to the chapter *Audit Value* in *Volume I* of *Driving Audit Value*, where the customer value proposition was discussed. The audit function performs its duties in order to provide the added value to its customers. The customers decide what added value is to them. When working in a company with many compliance issues, weak internal control systems, or numerous issues in financial reporting, it is logical that executive management and the board will want the audit function to focus on these topics, because that is added value to them. Entering into a discussion why the primary focus of the annual audit plan should be on a different subject (for example a business topic), would not do the credibility and reputation any good in such a case. This means that the CAE needs to strike a good balance in his audit plan; a balance between the low-level groundwork for the internal control systems and the high-level business topics. In case of doubt, have another look at the chapter about the annual audit planning in *Volume I* of *Driving Audit Value*, particularly the section about the calibration of the annual audit plan.

Audit Risk 3: Execution Risks

Figure 27 – Fourteen Elements of Execution Risk

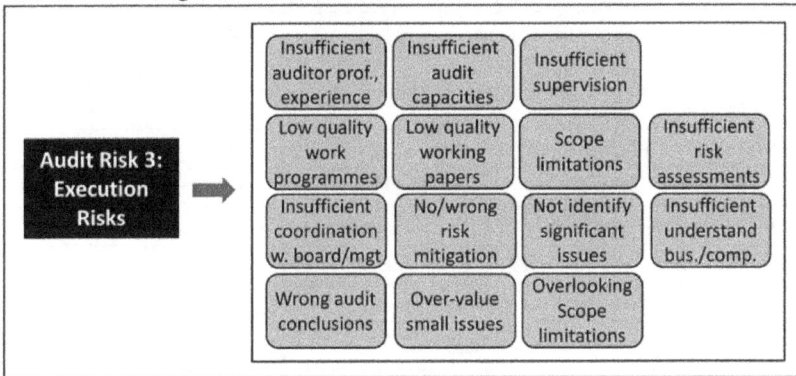

Audit Risk 3: Execution Risks ➡	Insufficient auditor prof., experience	Insufficient audit capacities	Insufficient supervision	
	Low quality work programmes	Low quality working papers	Scope limitations	Insufficient risk assessments
	Insufficient coordination w. board/mgt	No/wrong risk mitigation	Not identify significant issues	Insufficient understand bus./comp.
	Wrong audit conclusions	Over-value small issues	Overlooking Scope limitations	

The execution risk is the risk that the annual audit plan is not properly developed and implemented, or the audit engagements are not executed in a proper way, for achieving the customer value proposition.

In the following Execution Risk Matrix, the 14 execution risks from the *Audit Risks Catalogue*© are matched with the three execution objectives from the *Audit Objectives Catalogue*©. In the Execution Risk Map, the 14 execution risks are mapped to the audit function's customer value proposition. The conclusions from this matrix and map are:

- Nine of the 14 risks apply to all three objectives. This means that the majority of the execution risks can occur in the annual audit planning as well as the individual audit engagements.

- Six execution risks have a high likelihood and impact on the customer value proposition.

Figure 28 – Execution Risk Matrix

EXECUTION RISK MATRIX			
Execution Objectives: Execution Risks:	EO-1: Annual audit planning	EO-2: Audit engage-ments	EO-3: Follow-up and progress engage-ments
ER-1: Insufficient auditor proficiency/experience	✓	✓	✓
ER-2: Insufficient audit capacities	✓	✓	✓
ER-3: Insufficient supervision	✓	✓	✓
ER-4: Low quality work programmes	✓	✓	✓
ER-5: Low quality working papers	✓	✓	✓
ER-6: Scope limitations	✓	✓	✓
ER-7: Insufficient coordination with the board/management	✓	✓	✓
ER-8: Insufficient risk assessments	✓	✓	✓
ER-9: Insufficient understanding of the business and company	✓	✓	✓
ER-10: Not identify significant issues, when they do exist		✓	✓
ER-11. No or wrong audit issue risk mitigation measures		✓	✓
ER-12: Wrong audit engagement conclusions		✓	✓
ER-13: Over-value small audit engagement issues		✓	✓
ER-14: Overlooking audit engagement scope limitations		✓	✓

Figure 29 – Execution Risk Map

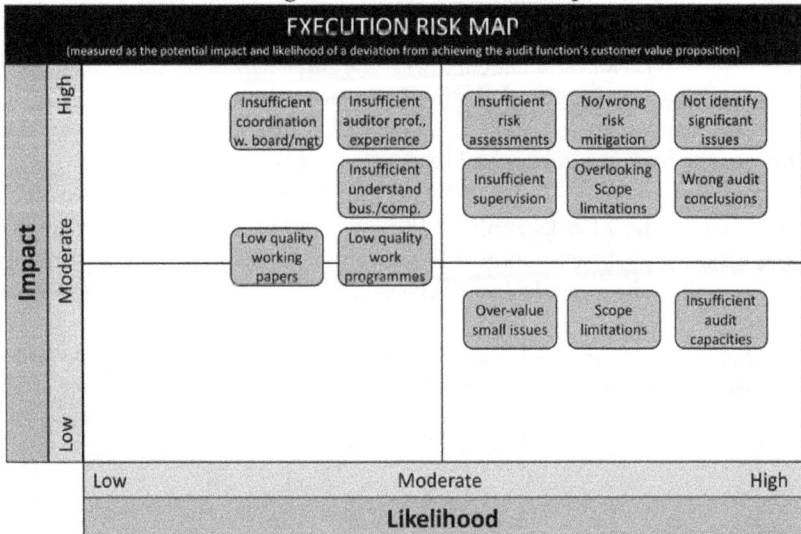

EXECUTION RISK MAP
(measured as the potential impact and likelihood of a deviation from achieving the audit function's customer value proposition)

The chapter is divided into six sections:
1. Risk of poor execution (ER-1 to 9)
2. Risk of overlooking significant issues (ER-10)
3. Risk of agreeing no or wrong audit issue risk mitigation measures (ER-11)
4. Risk of wrong audit engagement conclusions (ER-12)
5. Risk of over-valuing small issues (ER-13)
6. Risk of overlooking scope limitations (ER-14)

Risk of poor execution

Definition

The risk of poor execution is the probability that the audit function's general internal processes are of too low a quality to achieve the relevant audit objectives. These general internal processes relate to: insufficient understanding of the business; insufficient risk assessments; insufficient coordination with management and the board; insufficient experience and proficiency of the auditors and CAE; insufficient working paper documentation; insufficient supervision; and insufficiently tailored work programmes.

Examples

Unexpected reductions in the audit resources may lead to limitations in the audit capacities, as a result of which the annual audit plan cannot be completely implemented, or the duration of an audit needs to be cut short. Scope limitations may arise when management limits the access to critical information or people during the development of the annual audit plan or the performance of the audit engagement. Each audit engagement has specific audit assurance objectives. In the case of generic work programmes, the auditors might not know what to do exactly to reach the audit objective. Similarly, when the working paper documentation is limited, the CAE may not be able to draw the correct audit conclusions. When the CAE has no time to supervise the audit results, she might miss the fact that the auditor only executed part of the work programme.

Causes

These generic risks may be caused by insufficient quality or standardisation of the audit processes and procedures, insufficient proficiency and development of the auditors, and short term audit capacity issues. Scope limitations, caused by non-access to subject matter information and people, could be caused by a wrong audit time scheduling or a bad reputation of the audit function.

Impact on audit function

The generic execution risks may result in the audit function's inability to reach the objectives of the annual audit plan or the audit engagements, thereby reducing the value of the audit activities.

Impact on process owner

In most cases, the auditee, process owner and lower management will not care about the audit function's shortfall on their own audit objectives. Most of these generic execution risks are audit function internal risks, which are usually not visible to local management. They are indifferent to the fact that the audit function's end products (annual audit plan or audit engagement reports) do not achieve the expectations of the CAE, executive management or the board. Only when they receive a very negative audit report, although they believe that no significant issues are present, will they enter into discussions to invalidate the results of the audit work.

Impact on division/business unit management

Division/business unit management's reaction will be similar to the process owner and local management.

Impact on executive management and audit committee/board

Executive management and the board have no visibility on or interest in the audit function's internal processes. They do expect the CAE to achieve the audit objectives, and leave it up to her to organise the audit function in an appropriate manner. This gives the CAE a lot of freedom, but also responsibility. In case executive management and the board determine that the audit function does not achieve its objectives any more, they will initiate discussions to understand the causes. These discussions should then lead to improvements of the internal processes (for example through the quality assurance and improvement programme and the periodic quality assessments).

Risk drivers

The following risk drivers have a major influence on the level of the generic execution risks, and the lower each of these elements, the higher the risk:

- The level of quality or standardisation of the audit processes and procedures.
- The proficiency and development of the auditors.

- The short-term audit capacity issues.

The higher each of these elements, the higher the risk:
- The level of challenge of achieving the audit objectives.
- The complexity of the subject matter.
- The level of ambiguity, judgement and estimates to achieve objectives within the processes of the subject matter.

Determining risk levels

High generic execution risks may occur when: the audit function processes are not standardised and of low quality; working with inexperienced auditors whose skills are not further developed; the audit function does not manage short-term capacity shortfalls; the subject matters have high inherent risk; audit objectives are very challenging.

Low generic execution risks may occur when: the audit function processes are standardised and of high quality; working with experienced auditors whose skills are further developed; the audit function manages short-term capacity shortfalls; the subject matters have low inherent risk; audit objectives are easily attainable.

Risk of overlooking significant issues

Definition

The risk of overlooking the significant issues during the audit engagement is the probability that significant issues in the subject matter are not identified, whereas risks of significant deviations from achieving the subject matter's objectives are present. As a consequence, the CAE issues a clean, satisfactory, unqualified audit opinion/report, without reporting any significant issues, although significant issues do exist in the audited subject matter.

Examples

The auditors perform a review of the internal controls relating to the SAP user rights for the FI/CO module, particularly the automated payment module, and come to the conclusion that all the user rights are well controlled. They have no significant issues to report, and the CAE issues a clean audit opinion. However, the auditors overlooked the fact that there are a number of system administrators, who have a direct, unlogged, and unlimited access to the underlying Oracle databases, while using a generic group username sharing the software provider's default system password.

Causes

The CAE issues an unqualified audit report, without reporting any significant issues, whereas significant issues do exist in the audited subject matter. This means that the CAE was not aware that her auditor, her audit team, or she herself overlooked significant issues. The auditor or the audit team might not be aware, or they might actually be aware, but not tell the CAE or have not documented it in the working papers. Another possibility is that the relevant issue was identified and reported, but it was not considered to be significant in the CAE's, her team's or management's judgement. In such a case, there is a judgement error. When the CAE is not aware of something that she, however, should have known, the effectiveness of her supervision process is doubtful. When the CAE knows about the issue but does not consider it significant, whereas it is, her judgement process is doubtful. The result of not knowing or wrongly judging is that the CAE issues a positive internal audit report, whereas it should have been negative.

Impact on audit function

If it is never discovered, or reported, that the audit function missed the significant issues, the CAE's reputation with executive management and the board remains intact. However, their satisfaction (with the quality of local management) will turn into a dissatisfaction (with the quality of the audit execution) if they would later find out that internal audit overlooked or misjudged important issues. Such a discovery could be triggered by several events: local management themselves might come forward when they cannot contain the problems anymore; division/business unit management might find out after a deep-dive to review business or transaction anomalies; the external auditor might identify it; or the compliance function, risk management function, legal department or another corporate or local function might find out. Once this is out, it will come back to the CAE, and then she will need to take actions to prevent a permanent damage to her reputation and the credibility of the audit function.

Impact on process owner

In most cases, the auditee, process owner and lower management will not mind. They prefer to see a positive audit report rather than a negative one, as it makes them look better towards higher management and the board. When there are significant issues in the subject matter, it is very likely that the auditee, the process owner and responsible management are aware of these. It is really seldom that the operational people are not aware of the big problems in their area of responsibility. But these people have a financial incentive (bonus) and reputation risk that they want to protect and therefore are unlikely to come forward with a message that the auditor overlooked or misinterpreted a significant issue. They might even pride themselves that they were able to hide something from the auditor. They might leave the issue as it is, or they might start cleaning it up, because they might not be so lucky during the next audit visit. The local process owner might think that the auditor can be easily fooled.

Impact on division/business unit management

Division/business unit management's reaction could go either way. A business unit leader who values the identification of the significant issues over the possible negative impact on his reputation as a leader, will want the audit function to identify the big issues during their audit engagements. Such a leader will want the auditors to identify and address the important risks in the subject matter. To the contrary, a business unit leader who wants to make sure that he receives audit reports without significant issues, will probably keep his mouth shut. He might think that the audit function should concentrate on the basic process controls, whereas he will continue to address and manage the significant risks in his business. He might even think that it should not be within the mandate of the audit function to review the important business issues.

Impact on executive management and audit committee/board

Executive management and the board do want the audit function to identify significant issues when they exist in the subject matter under audit. They will want to know. But when the CAE does not report any such issues, they will trust that the subject matter is indeed free from significant issues, and they will be satisfied with the result.

Risk drivers

The following risk drivers have a major influence on the level of risk of overlooking significant issues, and the lower each of these elements, the higher the risk:

- The focus, depth and width of the audit testing programme.
- The quality of the working paper documentation.
- The effectiveness of the internal audit supervision processes.
- The quality of the auditor/audit manager/CAE.
- The auditors' and the CAE's capability to think like a business manager.

- The level of access to critical information and the value driving aspects of the subject matter.

The higher each of these elements, the higher the risk:
- The complexity of the subject matter.
- The level of ambiguity, judgement and estimates to achieve objectives within the processes of the subject matter.

Generally, the higher the inherent risks and the control risks of the company, the subject matter, or the audit function, the higher the risk of overlooking significant issues.

Determining risk levels

The audit engagement process has a high risk of overlooking significant issues when: supervision and working paper documentation processes are weak or absent; working with newly recruited inexperienced auditors; the audit testing programmes are generic, not tailored to the subject matter being audited; auditing topics that have a high inherent risk and a high control risk.

The audit engagement process has a low risk of overlooking significant issues when: supervision and quality control processes are formalised and effective; qualified and experienced auditors conduct the audit; the audit testing programme is tailor made to the risk profile of the subject matter; the subject matter has a low inherent risk and a low control risk.

Risk of agreeing no or wrong audit issue risk mitigation measures

Definition

The risk of agreeing no or wrong audit issue risk mitigation measures during the audit engagement is the probability that the audit function does not identify the correct measures that mitigate those identified risks, or that those measures are not agreed with the process owner. The latter could occur when the audit methodology is to provide recommendations to management, but leaves open what exact risk mitigation will actually be implemented by management.

Examples

The auditors identify that foreign customers purchase spare parts packages together with the machines, but that many customers ask to return those spare parts packages subsequent to the sales transaction, and that the refunds are often collected in cash by those foreign customers. Wrong risk mitigations would be:

- Recognising that this is an acceptable industry practice; hence no risk mitigation is demanded.
- Only making a recommendation that no refunds in cash should be made anymore, but leaving it up to management to decide how they will exactly do this.
- Agreeing with management that they should not make any refunds at all, by stipulating this in their terms and conditions of sale.
- Agreeing with management to only accept the returned spare parts packages at discounted prices.

Causes

The risk of agreeing no or wrong audit issue risk mitigation measures during the audit engagement could be triggered by the audit methodology of making recommendations but not agreeing on the exact risk mitigation to be initiated by management. In my personal view this is basically only doing half the work. The risk could also be triggered by insufficient understanding of the business, insufficient experience and proficiency of the auditors or insufficient understanding of the involved risks.

Impact on audit function

Agreeing no or wrong audit issue risk mitigation measures has a direct impact on the achievement of the customer value proposition. The main purpose of the audit function is to support the board and management in achieving their objectives by identifying risks and initiating the mitigation of these risks. Identifying the risks but not initiating the correct or complete mitigations results in the risks continuing to exist. This diminishes the added value of the audit function.

Impact on process owner

The auditee, process owner and lower management want to mitigate their risks. Usually they are highly appreciative of concrete suggestions from the audit function on how to reduce their risks. In my personal experience, most managers do not just want the auditors to identify a problem, but want them to provide a risk reduction solution at the same time. These solutions need to be cost- and time-effective, and fit within their process flows and business model. For them the efficiency and effectiveness of the mitigation measures play an important role. They are under pressure to deliver business performance (sales, profits, cost savings) and additional risk mitigation actions will probably take time away from their operational activities. For this reason, the audit function must make sure that their suggested and agreed mitigation measures are highly efficient and effective. Particularly for inexperienced auditors this is quite a challenge.

I have experienced process owners who strongly influenced the risk mitigation measures documented in the audit report, but also managers who just accepted whatever the auditors wrote, even when they did not agree with it. For the quality of the audit results it is far better to have an intensive discussion, then a manager who accepts but silently disagrees. This is why I always triggered discussions on the risk mitigations, even when management did not oppose to the suggestions. Quite often this did result in a valuable fine-tuning of the risk reduction measures.

Impact on division/business unit management

Division/business unit management expect the audit function to initiate the risk mitigations together with the risk identifications. They expect the auditors to understand their business priorities and adjust the risk reduction measures to their business processes. No risk mitigation, or inefficient or ineffective measures are not acceptable to these business leaders.

Impact on executive management and audit committee/board

Executive management and the board have the same view as divisional/business unit management. In many of my discussions with the company executives and the audit committee or board members, the focus was usually on four aspects of the significant issues: what is the issue, what was the root cause, what will be the risk mitigation, and by when will the risk be reduced to an acceptable level. For them the risk mitigation measures are an integral part of the mandate of the audit function.

Risk drivers

The following risk drivers have a major influence on the level of risk of agreeing no or wrong audit issue risk mitigation measures, and the lower each of these elements, the higher the risk:

- The auditors' and the CAE's capability to think like a business manager and their understanding of the business and risks.
- The experience and proficiency of the auditor/audit manager/CAE.
- The effectiveness of the internal audit supervision processes.

The higher each of these elements, the higher the risk:

* The complexity of the subject matter.
* The level of ambiguity, judgement and estimates to achieve objectives within the processes of the subject matter.

Determining risk levels

The audit engagement process has a high risk of agreeing no or wrong audit issue risk mitigation measures when: supervision is weak or absent; working with inexperienced auditors; auditing topics that have a high inherent risk; the auditor does not understand the business or the risks.

The audit engagement process has a low risk of agreeing no or wrong audit issue risk mitigation measures when: supervision and quality control processes are formalised and effective; qualified and experienced auditors conduct the audit; the subject matter has a low inherent risk; the auditors have a good understanding of the business, processes and risks; the auditors are able to think like a business manager.

Risk of wrong audit engagement conclusions

Definition

The risk of wrong audit engagement conclusions is the probability that the conclusions and audit opinion deviate from the facts. This risk may present itself in several forms:

* Overlooking significant issues: significant issues do exist in the subject matter, but the audit did not identify them. This is mostly an audit execution problem, as already described.

* Over-valuing small issues: small issues are considered to be significant issues. This is mostly an interpretation/perspective/judgement problem and is described in the next section of this chapter.

* Overlooking scope limitations: the audit conclusions are based on the expectation that the full audit work was performed, whereas a significant part of the audit work was not executed. This is mostly an internal communication/supervision problem and is described in the last section of this chapter.

- Wrong interpretation of the correct audit results: the audit results are factually correct, but their impact on the achievement of the audit objectives, subject matter objectives or the impact on the larger organisational units of the company, are falsely interpreted. This is mostly an interpretation/perspective/judgement problem and is described in this section.

Examples

The auditors identify that in 2 out of 20 samples from their process walk-through testing, the internal control system did not prevent the unapproved credit note to be released for payment to customers. They write as audit conclusion that the control is properly designed, and effective in its execution, as the related amounts were small. When the CAE does not supervise, or challenge this conclusion, she might not discover that: there are more than half a million credit notes, and the sample size is not representative to make a statement about the total population; these 2 exceptions relate to intercompany credit notes, which do not need advance approval; there are high value credit notes, not included in the testing, which may have been released without prior approval.

A local CFO approves bank payments with a single signatory, whereas the corporate policy prescribes double signatories. The auditor writes it up as a significant non-compliance issue and points out the high risk of fraud. When the CAE does not supervise, or challenge this conclusion, she might not discover that: business unit controlling is aware of the single signatory and as a compensating control keeps the local bank balance below $25'000 and reviews all the payments and withdrawals on a daily basis. As a result, the compliance issue continues to exist, but the risk of fraud is minimal.

The auditor identifies that the subsidiary in China has a 35 percent turnover rate of blue-colour factory workers. Local management explains that this is normal, as the workers with one year of experience can already command a 50 percent higher salary when they move to another company. It has been like this for years and in view of the growth of the local industrial park, the plant manager does not expect this competitive behaviour to stop any time soon. Thus, the auditor concludes that although it is unusual, there is nothing management can do about it, and no risk mitigation is possible and required. When the CAE does not supervise, or challenge this conclusion, she might not discover that: the business unit is embarking on a high growth strategy, and the 35 percent blue-colour turnover will significantly limit the local growth; corporate human resources has launched an initiative to stabilise the work force by ensuring remuneration in the highest quartile of the salary benchmark in all its businesses. Under both perspectives the issue is significant, and concrete risk mitigating actions need to be defined.

Causes

Wrong interpretation of the correct audit results may occur when; the results are assessed from a too narrow perspective; the auditor does not understand the business and company or the audit objective; the auditor is not aware of the latest business developments or is inexperienced in the subject matter under review. False conclusions may also be caused by haste: not taking enough time to deliberate on the facts and the results in the thought processes. At a company with a high inherent risk, the likelihood of false conclusions will be higher than in companies with a low inherent risk profile.

Impact on audit function

If it is never discovered, or reported, that the audit function made a false conclusion, the CAE's reputation with executive management and the board remains intact. However, they will be dissatisfied with the quality of the audit execution if they would later find out that internal audit made a serious judgement error.

Impact on process owner

The auditee, process owner and lower management will only feel affected by a false conclusion when the audit report is negative about their performance. In such a case, they will vehemently argue that the judgement of the auditor is wrong, as he does not consider all the circumstances, or the larger perspective of the business unit. In the case of a false positive or a neutral conclusion, they will not care: they will not tell the auditors that they are wrong and should write a negative audit opinion. They prefer to see a positive audit report rather than a negative one, as it makes them look better towards higher management and the board.

Impact on division/business unit management

Division/business unit management will principally want to receive audit reports that correctly interpret the audit results. In case they identify a false conclusion, because they have knowledge that the auditor does not have, they may keep silent when the report is positive (but should be negative), or they may reach out in case the report is negative (but should be neutral or positive). In the latter case, when the report is already formally distributed, they may inform executive management and the board of the misjudgement in the audit report. This will likely come back to the CAE, and she might be asked by executive management and the board to explain the differences in judgement.

Impact on executive management and audit committee/board

Executive management and the board expect the audit function to use appropriate judgement and consideration of multiple perspectives when writing the audit conclusions and opinions. They see it as the key role of the CAE to safeguard the fairness of the conclusions and to prevent any false conclusions. A single failure might not damage the reputation of the CAE, but repetitive false conclusions will.

Risk drivers

The following risk drivers have a major influence on the level of risk of a wrong interpretation of the correct audit results, and the lower each of these elements, the higher the risk:

- The ability to assess the subject matter and the results of the testing in the larger perspective of the higher organisational units.
- The effectiveness of the internal audit supervision processes.
- The quality of the auditor/audit manager/CAE.
- The auditors' and the CAE's capability to think like a business manager.
- The level of coordination of the audit results with the responsible managers.

The higher each of these elements, the higher the risk:

- The complexity of the subject matter.
- The level of ambiguity, judgement and estimates to achieve the objectives within the processes of the subject matter.

Determining risk levels

A high risk of a wrong interpretation of the correct audit results may occur when: supervision processes are weak or absent; working with inexperienced auditors; auditing topics that have a high inherent risk; there is no coordination of the audit results and conclusions with management; the auditors and the CAE have no business experience; the auditors and CAE are not able to assess the audit results in the larger perspective of the business.

A low risk of a wrong interpretation of the correct audit results may occur when: supervision and quality control processes are formalised and effective; qualified and experienced auditors conduct the audit; the subject matter has a low inherent risk; the CAE and auditors have a broad business perspective; the audit results are coordinated with the appropriate management levels.

Risk of over-valuing small issues

Definition

The risk of over-valuing small issues is the probability that issues are considered to be significant, whereas the subject matter actually contains only low or non-existent risks of deviations from achieving its objectives. The consequence is that the CAE issues a qualified audit report, reporting significant issues, whereas the issues are either not significant, or do not exist in the audited subject matter.

Examples

The audit team concludes that the internal controls over the expense reporting processes are very weak. They raise a significant issue about an expense reimbursement fraud. In the issued audit report, the CAE raises the red flag for the fraud risk. Subsequently, management together with the compliance team do a deep-dive, and it turns out that although the controls may be weak, there was no case of fraud. All the exceptions have valid explanations, though these were documented outside the expense report files.

Causes

This risk is based on a false interpretation of the facts (perhaps the facts were not complete or wrong), the circumstances or the relevance of the issue. In the perspective of the audit objective and management's subject matter objective, the potential impact of the identified risk exposure is factually lower than judged by the CAE and the auditor.

The audit function has the tendency to over-estimate the significance of the issues, whereas management has the tendency to under-estimate the impact and likelihood of the issues, when it comes to documenting this in an audit report. The auditor and the audit team tend to over-estimate the significance of the issues, because they do not have all the operational knowledge that the process owner has: they may lack the perspective, or the experience, in having the right judgement. Too often, the audit function wants to promote their own importance by showing audit results with a high significance. To the contrary, management has the tendency to under-estimate the significance of audit issues, to protect their reputation against a negative judgement on an area under their responsibility. It is the responsibility of the CAE to understand how her auditor or audit team came to their judgement, as well as to understand the line of thinking of responsible management. These are counter-balancing forces and the CAE needs to make up her own mind on the appropriate judgement on the significance of an issue when it is a topic of significant dispute.

Even when there is no dispute, the CAE still needs to form her own opinion. Any questions from executive management or the audit committee will come directly to her. Being professional means that she has the answer readily available when the question is raised. They know that the CAE released the report, so they expect her to be able to explain it, without any hesitation.

Impact on audit function

The result of the judgement error is that the CAE issues a negative internal audit report, whereas it should have been positive. Issues might actually exist, but because of an erroneous judgement, the CAE and the audit team blow these issues up, out of proportion, and out of perspective of the real underlying problem.

If the CAE over-values an issue that in reality is very small or non-existent, this is likely going to come back to her. Firstly, the CAE will be aware that the issue she reported as significant was controversial. Intensive discussions, within the team or with management, will have (hopefully) preceded the audit report completion. Secondly, the process owner or local management will not leave it at that. After the issuance of the internal audit report, they may lodge a complaint with their bosses, executive management, or directly with the board. I have experienced myself that a process owner sent an email expressing disagreement to everybody on the distribution list of my audit report, up to the chairman of the board. Suffice it to say that this was a bad experience to go through, with all the discussions that this email triggered. Thirdly, the board or executive management may ask the process owner for an explanation as to why they are not able to manage a significant issue in their business processes. Responsible management will then elaborately explain their view that there is really no issue, and that they tried everything to change the auditor's opinion, but that they would not listen. They will state that the audit function does not understand their business or does only half work, so that they did not have the proper perspective or all the facts. They are likely going to twist and turn to protect their own reputation and put the CAE in a bad light. This creates a lose-lose situation. The process owner has already been put in a negative light, and now so has the CAE. It is better to avoid this from happening, because when it does, the CAE will not be able to control the damage anymore. It is much better to control this process through her quality assurance processes and prevent an escalation.

The board and management may be aware that there could be differences of interpretation and differences in opinion about the impact and likelihood of the issues, but they expect the bare facts not to be disputed. In case of a significant difference of opinion, and the CAE still wants to report such issues, the outlet to express this difference of opinion should be available within the format/template of the audit report. Then executive management and the board can make up their own mind about the reported differences in opinion when they get presented the differing views. Not reporting significant differences in the judgement on the severity of the issues is not recommendable and should be avoided.

Impact on process owner

In the most cases, the auditee, process owner and lower management will try to do everything to prevent that a small issue is reported as significant. They prefer to see a positive report rather than a negative one, as it makes them look better towards the higher management and the board. They will enter into extensive discussions why the risks documented in the draft audit report are low instead of high, and will try to do everything to convince the CAE that her judgement is wrong. These people have a financial incentive (bonus) and a reputation risk that they want to protect and therefore are likely going to fight hard when they feel that an issue is assessed completely wrong. However, they might also fight hard in case a significant issue does exist. They might try to convince the CAE that the issue is small, which means that she cannot rely on the views expressed by the process owner only. The CAE and her auditors must also make up their own mind and really understand why management is fighting so hard against raising a topic as a significant issue. Is it politically motivated or fact based?

The only cases when the auditee, process owner and lower management will not try to talk the auditors out of their judgement of a significant issue is when they do not know any better themselves, when they are trying to use the audit report to procure more resources from senior management, or when they are setting the audit function up for failure. In such cases, the process owners' scrutiny to ensure an appropriate interpretation of the audit results does not work as a sanity check and safety net. Although these are considered exceptions, they do occur and I personally experienced this.

Impact on division/business unit and executive management

Division/business unit and executive management have the (spoken or unspoken) expectation that the CAE will have an appropriate judgement about the significance of the issues identified during an audit engagement. Generally, they do want the audit function to identify and report significant issues, but of course they do not want them to report such issues when they do not exist.

Impact on audit committee/board

The board has the same, spoken or unspoken, expectation of the CAE. When the CAE reports significant issues, they trust that she has discussed and agreed the facts of the problems with the relevant levels of management, including executive management, before they receive a copy of the audit report.

Risk drivers

The following risk drivers have a major influence on the level of the risk of over-valuing small issues, and the lower each of these elements, the higher the risk:

- The level of understanding of the subject matter and the issues.
- The coordination and agreement with the process owner and management.
- The quality of judgement to put the issues into perspective.
- The quality and experience of the CAE and the auditors.

Determining risk levels

The execution process has a high risk to over-value small issues as significant when: auditing topics that have a high inherent and control risk; the CAE and the auditors do not understand the subject matter; working with newly recruited inexperienced auditors; not knowing the perspective of executive management and the board; issuing the audit reports without quality control procedures; the audit results are not discussed with the process owner.

The execution process has a low risk to over-value small issues as significant when: the inherent risk and control risk of the subject matter are low; having a good understanding of the subject matter that is audited; working with qualified and experienced auditors; having formalised and effective quality control processes; knowing how executive management and the board think about relevant topics; having good issue coordination processes with the process owner.

Risk of overlooking scope limitations

Definition

The risk of overlooking scope limitations is the probability of issuing a full scope audit report, whereas a substantial part of the work on the subject matter has not been performed. The CAE issues an audit opinion/report on an audited subject matter, whereas she should not issue such an opinion/report because of the significant limitations in the audit scope or audit execution.

Examples

The audit engagement has the objective to provide assurance that the key internal controls over financial reporting are properly designed and operating effectively. During the audit scoping, the team assumes that there are no inventories, whereas inventories represent 50 percent of the assets on the balance sheet. As a consequence, the work programme does not include any audit work on the inventory controls, and no such audit work takes place. As a second example, the work programme does include the detailed testing of the inventory position. However, since the inventory documents are held at another location, the auditors are not able to execute these work programme steps, but do not inform the CAE about this. As a third example, the auditors want to perform their testing on the inventory position, however, the process owner refuses to cooperate and provide access to the documents. Whatever the cause, without good communication between the CAE and the auditors, the CAE runs the risk to issue a full scope assurance on the internal controls over financial reporting, whereas the most significant balance sheet position was outside the scope of their work.

Causes

This can only happen when either the audit scoping and/or the audit work programme was falling short of the objective of the audit (in the preparation phase), or when the auditor did not, or was not able to, perform the work as planned (in the execution phase). The results are, however, the same: the CAE provides management and the board with a false level of audit assurance.

The root cause for the shortfall in the preparation phase lies within the audit function. It could be caused by an insufficient understanding of the subject matter, or by insufficient time or knowledge to put together a focused work programme.

The root cause for the shortfall in the execution phase can lie within the audit function, as well as with the auditee or process owner. It has an internal cause when the auditor does not have enough time to work through all the audit steps, does not understand the steps, skips steps, or documents that work was done whereas nothing was done. It has a cause outside the audit function when the process owner cannot, or does not want to fulfil the time, data, or access requirements that the auditor needs to complete his work.

With respect to the internal causes, the CAE was not aware that her auditor, her audit team, or she herself overlooked shortfalls in the scoping, work programmes or execution of the audit work. If the CAE was aware of it, this scenario would not have arisen. When the CAE is not aware of something that she, however, should have known, the effectiveness of her supervision processes need to be questioned. With respect to the external cause, the auditor was not aware of the scope limitation, or chose to ignore it and did not escalate this within the audit function.

Impact on audit function

Whatever the cause, the result of not knowing the limitations, is that the CAE issued an internal audit report, which should probably not have been issued, or should have been issued with a scope restriction, and thus a restriction of the interpretation of the results of the audit engagement.
When the process owner does not complain about the false scope of the audit engagement report, it is unlikely that executive management or the board will find out. The only way they could be informed about the scope limitation is when subsequent to the audit significant (business, control or risk management) issues arise, which the audit engagement failed to identify because of the scope limitation. In such a case, damage may be done to the reputation and credibility of the audit function, commensurate the importance of the topic that was audited.

Impact on process owner

Generally, the auditee, process owner or local management, will not care too much, unless the report is very negative. Then they will try to manage it to the positive side by arguing that a significant part of the subject matter was left outside the audit, and had it been included, would have generated a completely different, i.e. positive, picture. There is a good chance that they escalate this through the management levels, up to executive management and even to the board, in the case of a very negative report.

Impact on division/business unit management

Division/business unit management's reaction could go either way. A business unit leader who values the work of the audit function expects an audit engagement report to properly represent the work performed. If this is not the case, he will receive a false level of security over the audited area. To the contrary, a business unit leader who wants to make sure that he receives audit reports without significant issues, will not care too much, unless the report is very negative.

Impact on executive management and audit committee/board

The board and executive management expect an audit engagement report to properly represent the work performed. If this is not the case, they will receive a false audit assurance, and they will receive a false level of security over the audited area. They expect the CAE to conclude on the work that actually was performed.

Risk drivers

The following risk drivers have a major influence on the level of the risk of issuing a full scope audit engagement report, whereas only partial audit work was performed, and the lower each of these elements, the higher the risk:

- The quality and coverage of the work programme and the completeness of the execution of the audit steps.
- The quality of the supervision processes and the working paper review.
- The completeness of the working paper documentation.
- The level of access to the data, information, transactions and process staff necessary for the completion of the audit testing.
- The quality of the communication between the auditor and the CAE.

Determining risk levels

The execution process has a high risk to overlook scope limitations when: engagement scoping is incomplete; generic work programmes are used; the subject matter of the audit is not understood; the subject matter of the audit is complex and spreads over multiple departments, entities or geographical locations; there is no supervision over the work performed; working paper documentation is poor; communication between the CAE and the auditor is limited.

The execution process has a low risk to overlook scope limitations when: the audit scoping is fine-tuned to the subject matter; detailed and focused work programmes are used; the subject matter is simple and small; working paper documentation is extensive; supervisory processes compare the work performed against the plan; communication between the CAE and the auditor is good.

Risk of doing much more audit work than needed

The above explanations all refer to overlooking scope limitations. There is of course also the other side of the coin: the risk of doing much more audit work than needed for achieving the objective of the audit. This risk is mostly an efficiency risk, as it does not necessarily have an impact on the quality of the assurance. When much more work is done than necessary to reach the audit objective, the CAE may incur this risk based on the absence of a focused work programme or a poor and untimely supervision process.

Audit Process Risks

Figure 30 – Three Audit Process Risk Categories

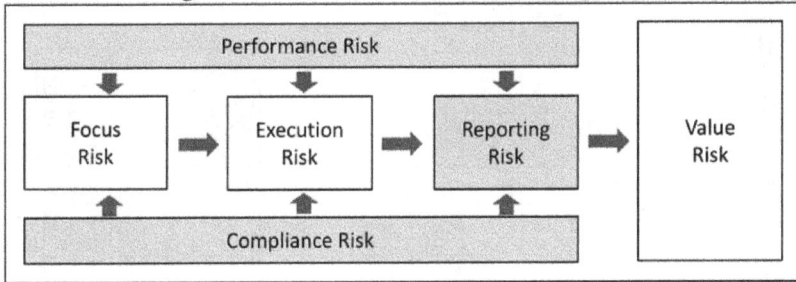

In the next three chapters, each of the three audit process risk categories, together with the 27 risks from the *Audit Risks Catalogue*©, are described and analysed in detail. The chapters have the following structure:

- A risk matrix matches the risks from the audit risks catalogue with the audit function objectives from the *Audit Objectives Catalogue*©.

- A risk map matches the risks from the audit risks catalogue with the achievement of the customer value proposition.

- The key conclusions from the risk matrix and risk map single out the topics for analysis and explanation. The selected topics are detailed in:
  - o defining the risk, followed by examples and an analysis of the causes;
  - o describing the impact of the risks on the audit function itself, as well as the impact from the perspective of the process owner, division/business unit management, executive management and the audit committee/board;
  - o analysing the risk drivers, as well as guidance for assessing the level of the risk.

Audit Process Risk Tree©

Figure 31 – Audit Process Risk Tree©

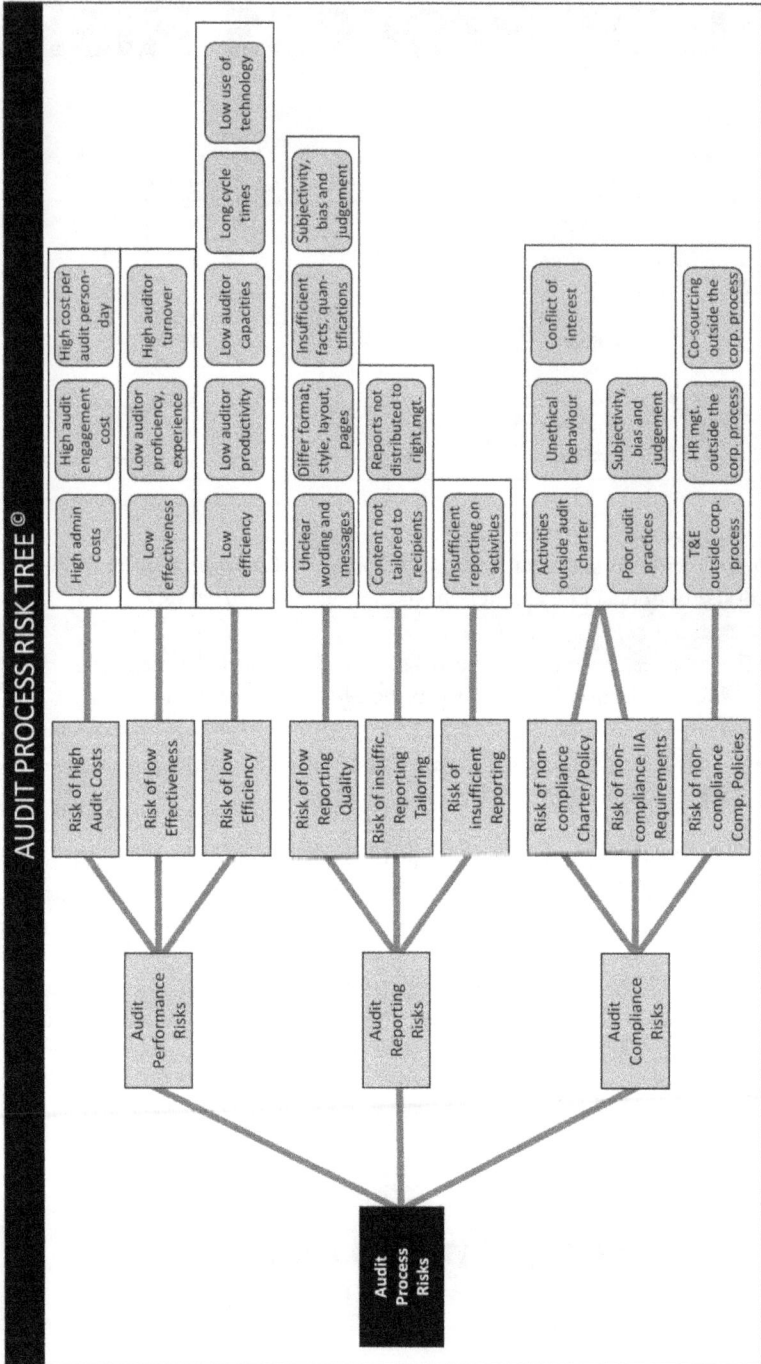

Audit Risk 4: Performance Risks

Figure 32 – Eleven Elements of Performance Risk

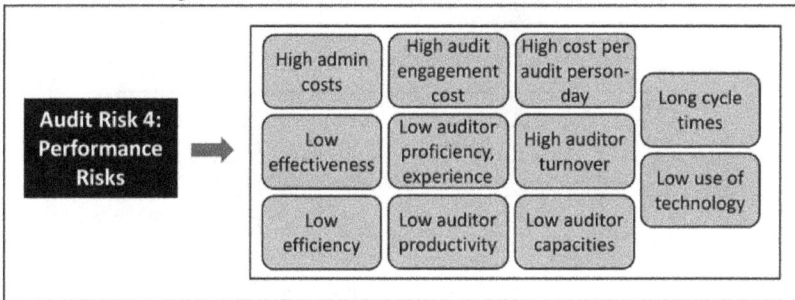

Audit Risk 4: Performance Risks	High admin costs	High audit engagement cost	High cost per audit person-day
	Low effectiveness	Low auditor proficiency, experience	High auditor turnover
	Low efficiency	Low auditor productivity	Low auditor capacities

Long cycle times

Low use of technology

The performance risk is the risk that the audit function processes and the use of the audit resources are not effective or efficient. Inefficiencies and ineffectiveness will endanger the achievement of the customer value proposition towards the board and management.

In the following Performance Risk Matrix, the 11 performance risks from the *Audit Risks Catalogue*© are matched with the four performance objectives from the *Audit Objectives Catalogue*©. In the Performance Risk Map, the 11 performance risks are mapped to the audit function's customer value proposition. The conclusions from this matrix and map are:

- Eight of the 11 risks apply to the people aspect of the audit function, making people the most important risk driver in the non-achievement of the performance objectives.

- Compared to the value, focus and execution risks, the individual performance risks have a relatively low impact on the achievement of the customer value proposition.

- Three risks relating to costs (price) can be clustered together, just as the three risks relating to effectiveness (product) and the five risks relating to efficiency (process).

Figure 33 – Performance Risk Matrix

PERFORMANCE RISK MATRIX				
Performance Objectives: / Performance Risks:	PO-1: Audit people	PO-2: Audit price (cost)	PO-3: Audit product	PO-4: Audit process
PR-1: High administrative costs	✓	✓		
PR-2: High audit engagement costs	✓	✓		
PR-3: High cost per audit person-day	✓	✓		
PR-4: Low effectiveness	✓		✓	
PR-5: Low auditor proficiency/experience	✓		✓	
PR-6: High auditor turnover	✓		✓	
PR-7: Low efficiency				✓
PR-8: Low auditor productivity	✓			✓
PR-9: Low auditor capacities	✓			✓
PR-10: Long cycle times				✓
PR-11: Low use of technology				✓

Figure 34 – Performance Risk Map

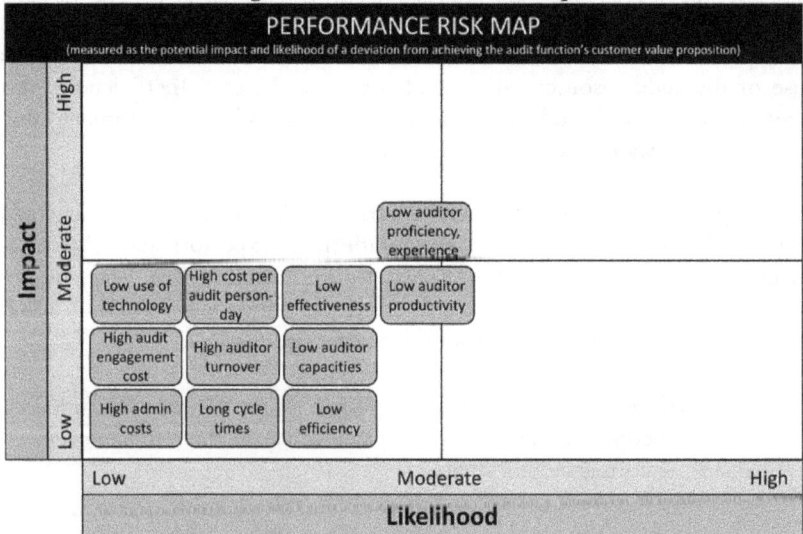

PERFORMANCE RISK MAP
(measured as the potential impact and likelihood of a deviation from achieving the audit function's customer value proposition)

The chapter is divided into three sections:
1. Risk of high audit costs (PR-1 to 3)
2. Risk of low effectiveness (PR-4 to 6)
3. Risk of low efficiency (PR-7 to 11)

Risk of high audit costs

Definition

The cost risk is the risk that the input – output ratio of the audit function is negative. In such a case, the cost of the audit function is too high compared to the perceived benefit.

Examples

The cost of the audit function is far above the budget, despite an even level of audit output. The average cost per audit person-day is much higher than the cost of outsourcing. The costs of the audit engagements are much higher than the value of the risks that are being identified. When purchasing co-sourcing audit services, the CAE does not make use of the rate discounts contained in the corporate contracts with the big four audit firms. The auditors travel in classes that are above the corporate standards.

Causes

The causes of the cost risk lie within the audit function. They may occur because the CAE does not; set productivity targets; manage productivity; make the costs of the audit activities transparent; approve travel and entertainment expense reports of the auditors.

Impact on audit function

If the CAE only manages the audit function based on the monthly budget of his cost centre, and executive management and the board only have this information as well, then it is rather unlikely that the financial consequences of low productivity and inefficiencies will be made visible. Executive management and the board may observe that an audit function of 15 auditors generates only 20 audit reports in a year, but without analysis, the underlying productivity issues may remain hidden within the audit function. A CAE who does not want transparency will probably be able to get away with this. Not managing the cost risk leaves the audit function and the CAE open to cost-cutting, resource reductions and ultimately outsourcing enforced by management or the board.

On the contrary, a CAE who maintains a performance management system and quantifies the costs of the audit person-days, audit engagements, administrative costs, and so forth, will have the possibility to pro-actively manage productivity and reduce his cost risk. He can use this as a tool to show executive management and the board how he is able to achieve the customer value proposition and increase the added value of the audit function by continuously monitoring and decreasing the cost levels until an optimum has been reached. Executive management and the board will recognise that the CAE thinks like a business manager and runs his audit function as a business, including the focus on the cost and productivity side of the activities.

Impact on process owner

The auditee, process owner or local management do not care about the cost of the audit function, as these are considered to be the costs of good corporate governance which they cannot influence. As long as these costs have no influence on their personal bonus achievement (for example due to recharging of the audit engagement costs which are included in their achievement calculations) they have no interest in it. Often times the costs of the audit engagements are not made transparent to local management.

Impact on division/business unit management

The same is valid for division/business unit management. They often regard the audit costs as non-controllable costs, and as long as these are excluded from their incentive calculation, they will be indifferent. However, this may change when these business leaders believe that their division is being allocated too high a share of the audit costs, when compared to the other divisions. They may complain to the CAE, to corporate controlling, or to the CFO or CEO.

Impact on executive management

If executive management perceives the cost of the audit function to be too high compared to the results of the audit work, they might let it go for a while. Depending on how busy they are with the other business topics, eventually, they will address it with the CAE. When the CEO and CFO believe that the audit function is not adding value, that it costs more than it yields, they may also develop an indifference to the audit work. They could think that they have no choice but to accept an audit function from the board's governance perspective, and they might just put the CAE, the audit function and the audit work results aside, as necessary but harmless.

Impact on audit committee/board

If the (chairman of the) audit committee believes that the audit function costs too much compared to its added value, they might ask the CAE some probing questions to get a better view as to what is causing the problem. If they do not get a good view of the problem or the root causes, they will enter into a discussion with executive management. They will ask the CEO or CFO to sort it out and come up with a proposal to improve the situation.

Risk drivers

The following risk drivers have a major influence on the level of cost risk, and the lower each of these elements, the higher the risk:

- The level of leverage of the audit cost.
- The level of transparency of the audit costs, for example by audit engagement and audit person-day.
- The level of the productivity and efficiency of the audit function.

Determining risk levels

The audit function has a high cost risk when: productivity of the auditors is low; there is no performance management system; the average cost per audit day is higher than the comparable costs of outsourcing.

The audit function has a low cost risk when: the CAE is actively managing productivity and performance; productivity is high; the average cost per audit day is far below the comparable costs of outsourcing.

Risk of low effectiveness

Definition

The risk of low effectiveness is the probability that the auditors are not doing the right things to reach the audit objectives. The quality of the output is lower than the target/expectations.

Examples

An auditor is tasked to provide reasonable assurance that all the 10'000 credit notes have been approved by the proper management levels. He takes the binder with the copies of the credit notes and starts reviewing the signatories on the individual pages for a sample of 100. However, the CAE questions whether the sample of 100 is sufficient to make a statement about 10'000 documents. The CAE suggests that the auditor uses the ERP system to check the electronic approval in the document work flow management system. From the system, he can print a listing of the credit notes that do not have an approval. Testing 100 percent of the population (in an efficient way) is a much more effective method to reach the audit objective.

Though this example shows a process aspect, it is the auditor's insufficient proficiency which triggered the ineffectiveness.

Causes

Low effectiveness may by caused by an absence of clear goals, a lack of information needed to reach the goals, insufficient communication or absence of performance feedback. Auditors unfamiliar with the technical audit work or the subject matter may also have lower effectiveness.

Impact on audit function

Low effectiveness has a direct impact on the achievement of the customer value proposition and the audit objectives of the engagements. When the CAE wants the low effectiveness to be compensated by additional audit work, it will increase the inefficiency. But if the CAE wants to achieve the audit objectives and customer value proposition, the effectiveness will receive a higher priority than the efficiency.

Impact on process owner

Generally, the level of effectiveness of the auditors has no impact on the auditee, process owner and lower management. Only when the low effectiveness results in the redoing of audit work, will the process owner be impacted by having to spend increased time with the auditor. Though the process owner will probably not be aware of the reasons. In case of a very low effectiveness, the audit objective might not be reached, but local management will not care about that.

Impact on division/business unit management

The impact on division/business unit management is principally the same as described for the process owner.

Impact on executive management and audit committee/board

Executive management and the board do want the audit function to be effective in their activities. Only through a high level of effectiveness will the audit function be able to achieve the customer value proposition and add value to the company and business.

Risk drivers

The following risk drivers have a major influence on the level of effectiveness, and the lower each of these elements, the higher the risk:

- The focus, depth and width of the audit testing programme.
- The effectiveness of the internal audit supervision processes.
- The proficiency and experience of the auditor/audit manager/CAE.

The higher each of these elements, the higher the risk:

- The complexity of the subject matter.
- The level of ambiguity, judgement and estimates to achieve objectives within the processes of the subject matter.

Determining risk levels

A high risk of low effectiveness occurs when: supervision and feedback processes are weak or absent; working with inexperienced auditors; the audit testing programmes are generic, not tailored to the subject matter being audited; auditing topics that have a high inherent risk.

A low risk of low effectiveness occurs when: supervision and feedback processes are formalised and effective; qualified and experienced auditors conduct the audit; the audit testing programme is tailor made to the risk profile of the subject matter; the subject matter has a low inherent risk.

Risk of low efficiency

Definition

The risk of low efficiency is the probability that the auditors are not conducting the audit activities in an as short as possible time. The quantity of the output is lower than the target/expectations.

Examples

An auditor needs to review the fixed assets additions by vouching the value in the accounts to the underlying purchase invoices. He searches through 40 purchasing binders to find the 10 relevant invoices. His efficiency would have been much higher if he identified the invoice numbers from the ledger, and then searched the 10 vouchers he was looking for.

The auditor writes his findings in a word document, and in a separate document develops the audit report. Audit automation software would enable a higher efficiency, as audit reports can be built automatically from the integrated working papers.

The auditors write the audit report after completion of the field work, once they are back in the office. Due to remote communications with the process owner, however, the completion of the audit report takes 3 days more and 7 days longer than when the report would have been written during the field work. This results in inefficiencies and a longer cycle time.

Causes

Low efficiency may by caused by demotivation, chaotic work and planning, absence of focus, absence of feedback and lack of pressure (deadlines). Low productivity may be caused by an absence of performance management and the low use of technology.

Impact on audit function

Low efficiency means that the resources produce less output than expected. Since the largest part of the audit function's resources are people, efficiency at the audit function level can be steered though capacity planning and audit scheduling. At the audit engagement level, it can be steered through clear work programmes and audit automation for documentation, supervision and reporting. Low efficiency would mean that the audit function generates less audit reports than it could, and that each audit report may take longer, or use more resources, for its completion. If the CAE sets no efficiency and productivity standards, he cannot be sure that the annual audit plan can indeed be fully implemented. He may fall short of the target to fully implement the audit plan. Inefficiencies in the audit engagements may lead to overlap of projects or postponement of subsequent engagements.

Impact on process owner

Generally, the level of efficiency of the auditors has no impact on the auditee, process owner and lower management. Only when the low efficiency results in extension of the audit field work, will the process owner be impacted by having to spend increased time with the auditor. Though the process owner will probably not be aware of the reasons.

Impact on division/business unit management

The impact on division/business unit management is principally the same as described for the process owner.

Impact on executive management and audit committee/board

Executive management and the board want the audit function to be efficient in their activities. Only through a high level of efficiency will the audit function be able to achieve the customer value proposition as it maximises the output of the audit resources.

Risk drivers

The following risk drivers have a major influence on the level of efficiency, and the lower each of these elements, the higher the risk:

- The level of the performance targets and the productivity (available audit days) of the auditors.
- The standardisation and automation of the internal audit processes.
- The proficiency and experience of the auditor/audit manager/CAE.

Determining risk levels

A high risk of inefficiency occurs when: performance targets are not set and performance is not measured; all audit processes are manual; audit processes are not standardised; the auditors are not experienced.

A low risk of inefficiency occurs when: performance targets are challenging and performance is frequently measured; all audit processes are automated; audit processes are standardised; the auditors are experienced.

Audit Risk 5: Reporting Risks

Figure 35 – Eight Elements of Reporting Risk

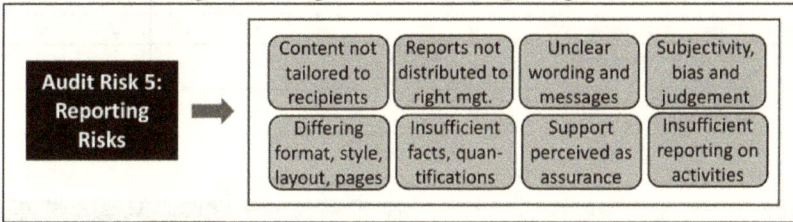

Audit Risk 5: Reporting Risks	Content not tailored to recipients	Reports not distributed to right mgt.	Unclear wording and messages	Subjectivity, bias and judgement
	Differing format, style, layout, pages	Insufficient facts, quantifications	Support perceived as assurance	Insufficient reporting on activities

The reporting risk is the risk that the audit reporting does not accurately and completely reflect the audit function's activities and the achievement of the customer value proposition.

In the following Reporting Risk Matrix, the eight reporting risks from the *Audit Risks Catalogue*© are matched with the seven reporting objectives from the *Audit Objectives Catalogue*©. In the Reporting Risk Map, the eight reporting risks are mapped to the audit function's customer value proposition. The conclusions from this matrix and map are:

- Six of the eight risks apply to all seven reporting requirements. This means that all the types of reports are subject to these same generic risk exposures.

- Reports not distributed to the right management, and content not tailored to the recipients, are two risks that need input from the customers. These risks have the highest impact.

Figure 36 – Reporting Risk Matrix

Reporting Risks: \ Reporting Objectives:	RO-1: Audit committee reporting	RO-2: Audit Performance reporting	RO-3: Annual reporting of the audit function	RO-4: Annual audit plan reporting	RO-5: Audit engagement reporting	RO-6: Progress reporting	RO-7: Knowledge sharing reporting
REPORTING RISK MATRIX							
RR-1: Content not tailored to the recipients	✓	✓	✓	✓	✓	✓	✓
RR-2: Reports not distributed to the right management	✓	✓	✓	✓	✓	✓	✓
RR-3: Unclear wording and messages	✓	✓	✓	✓	✓	✓	✓
RR-4: Differing format, style, layout, too many pages	✓	✓	✓	✓	✓	✓	✓
RR-5: Insufficient facts and quantifications	✓	✓	✓	✓	✓	✓	✓
RR-6: Subjectivity, bias and judgement	✓	✓	✓	✓	✓	✓	✓
RR-7: Insufficient reporting on the audit function activities	✓	✓	✓	✓			
RR-8: Audit support or consulting work being perceived as audit assurance work	✓		✓	✓			

Figure 37 – Reporting Risk Map

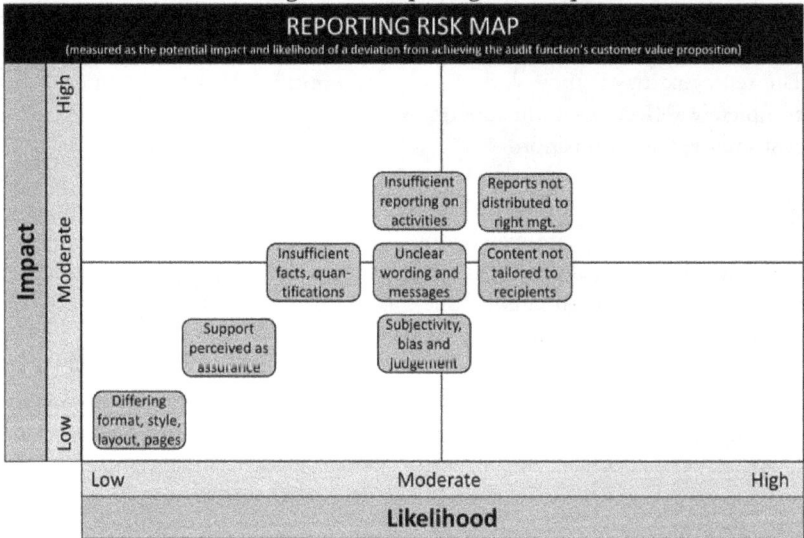

The chapter is divided into three sections:

1. Risk of low reporting quality (RR-3 to 6)
2. Risk of insufficient reporting tailoring (RR-1 and 2)
3. Risk of insufficient reporting (RR-7 and 8)

Risk of low reporting quality

Definition

The risk of low reporting quality is the likelihood that reports have: unclear wording and messages; differing formats, style, layout; insufficient facts and quantifications; too many pages; bias and judgement.

Examples

Audit reports may have extensive process and control descriptions to support the audit findings, resulting in more than 120 pages. The audit department does not have a report template. As a result of which, the style of wording, formats and lay-outs are different among the auditors who write the reports. The wording of the issues in the audit report is mostly based on the auditor's view of what is "right" and "wrong". These descriptions are not supported by the basic facts and quantifications relating to the subject matter under review. A new auditor is not used to business writing and has difficulties expressing himself in the English language. As a result of which, the audit issues are difficult to understand.

Causes

The causes fully relate to the audit function's internal processes: the level of standardisation and the clarity of the product requirements. These generic reporting risks may occur when the CAE does not set clear performance standards and does not standardise the audit reports, writing styles, and so forth. Particularly inexperienced auditors may have difficulties in writing clear messages and avoiding bias and judgement in their conclusions and process descriptions.

Impact on audit function

These generic reporting risks are occurring in the interfaces with the audit customers. This means that management and the board are directly impacted when such risks occur. The result is either one of two reactions back to the audit function: no reaction, as they do not understand and ignore the reports; a negative reaction, complaining that they cannot understand the reports and conclusions. Reputation and credibility will be damaged, and it is unlikely that the customer value proposition will be achieved.

Impact on process owner

Generally, the auditee, process owner or local management, will not care too much about the number of pages, format, layout and wording in the audit report. Their sensitivity will be heightened in case of bias and wrong judgement, when they believe that they receive an unfair negative audit report. Then they will try to manage it to the positive side by arguing that the auditors are biased and use a wrong judgement in concluding on the audit issues. They may state that the numbers and quantifications would show a different picture, but that such critical data was omitted from the audit report. There is a good chance that local management escalates the auditor's perceived bias and wrong judgement through the management levels, up to executive management and even to the board in case of a very negative report.

Impact on division/business unit management

Division/business unit management's reaction will be the same as the process owner and local management.

Impact on executive management and audit committee/board

The board and executive management expect the CAE to provide them with reports that are crystal clear on the facts and conclusions, and easy to understand. If this is not the case, they may either ignore the reports or start a feedback process to the CAE.

Risk drivers

The following risk drivers have a major influence on the reporting quality, and the lower each of these elements, the higher the risk:
- The level of standardisation of the reports and reporting processes.
- The quality of the supervision processes.
- The experience of the auditors and CAE.
- The quality and standardisation of the performance management.

Determining risk levels

The reporting processes have a high quality risk when: no performance standards have been set; the CAE and the auditors have little experience in writing the audit reports; the audit reporting requirements have not been standardised and explicitly determined; there is no supervision over the report writing.

The reporting processes have a low quality risk when: the audit reporting requirements are defined and standardised; the auditors are experienced in writing business reports; the CAE has elaborate discussions with the auditors about understanding and formulating the critical elements in the audit reports.

Risk of insufficient reporting tailoring

Definition

The risk of insufficient reporting tailoring is the likelihood that the reports have content that is not tailored to the recipients, or that the reports are not distributed to the right recipients.

Examples

Audit reports may have extensive process and control descriptions to support the audit findings, resulting in more than 120 pages. These full audit reports are distributed to all levels of management and the audit committee. Executive management and the board members do not receive extracts with only the key messages.

Although serious compliance issues have been identified in a subsidiary, the CAE does not provide the corporate compliance function a copy of the audit report.

Causes

The causes fully relate to the audit function internal processes: the level of understanding of the information requirements from the key customers, including the 1st and 2nd lines of defence.

Impact on audit function

These reporting risks are occurring in the interfaces with the audit customers. The audit function wants to profile itself as a well-established department with many connections and relations into the 1st and 2nd lines of defence. For this reason, failing to report important audit results to an important stakeholder may result in criticism from this stakeholder. Such an ad-hoc reporting oversight is, however, easy to rectify and will normally not have any impact on the achievement of the customer value proposition (unless the key customers are systematically excluded from reporting).

Impact on process owner

Generally, the auditee, process owner or local management, will not care about the tailoring of the report content to their needs. Usually, they accept whatever audit report format and content structure is produced by the audit function. Local management will normally critically review the distribution list of the audit reports, to ensure that their direct supervisors and the higher levels of management are included. In case of a very negative report, they may try to convince the auditor to limit the distribution list.

Impact on division/business unit management

Division/business unit management's reaction will be the same as the process owner or local management.

Impact on executive management and audit committee/board

The board and executive management expect the CAE to provide them with reports that are tailored to their needs of receiving audit assurance and focusing on the critical issues. If this is not the case, they may either ignore the reports or start a feedback process to the CAE.

Risk drivers

The following risk drivers have a major influence on the level of this reporting tailoring risk, and the lower each of these elements, the higher the risk:

- The level of understanding of the customer reporting requirements.
- The level of standardisation of the distribution lists.
- The level of understanding of the management structures.

Determining risk levels

The reporting processes have a high reporting tailoring risk when: the audit reporting requirements and distribution lists have not been standardised and explicitly determined; the CAE and auditors do not understand the management structures.

The reporting processes have a low reporting tailoring risk when: the audit reporting requirements are defined and standardised in coordination with the key customers; the CAE and auditors have a good understanding of the management structures.

Risk of insufficient reporting

Definition

The risk of insufficient reporting on the audit function activities is the probability that the CAE does not show all the critical activities that lead to the fulfilment of the customer value proposition to executive management and the board. This risk relates to the reporting, to the audit committee/board and executive management, of the focus and results of the audit assurance work as well as the support or consulting work.

Insufficient reporting about the support and consulting work may lead the board and management to falsely believe that audit assurance was provided.

Examples

The CAE does not prepare an annual report for the audit function, so she does not show how the results of the audit work during the past calendar year contributed to the mitigation of the company's business risks. The audit function does not maintain a balanced scorecard, hence critical performance information on productivity, audit cycle times, cost of audit person-days, and so forth, are not communicated to the key stakeholders of the audit function. The IT auditor spends six weeks supporting the roll-out and implementation of a new ERP system. Though no audit work was performed, the board believes that they receive audit assurance because the CAE issued a report in the same format as the audit assurance report. Or perhaps the CAE did not issue a report, but the key customers still believe that assurance was provided as no communication to the contrary was received.

Causes

On the one hand, the CAE may not know or understand the reporting requirements from her key customers, on the other hand she might have insufficient experience or creativity in capturing the main elements of the performance of the audit function. If the CAE issues a report of the support work, in the same format and structure as the audit assurance reports, the recipients of the report may easily be confused into thinking that it related to an audit assurance assignment.

Impact on audit function

If the CAE does not provide executive management and the board with a comprehensive report on the activities and results of the audit function, she will have difficulties in pointing the attention of these business leaders to the added value of her activities. This could result in an under-valuation of the audit department. The risk of insufficient reporting on the audit function activities is mostly not seizing an opportunity. It is the opportunity for the CAE to make transparent, market and promote the value of the audit function, and show the leaders of the company what excellent contributions were provided in helping the business become successful.

What if the holistic reporting shows that the overall contribution and performance are below the expectations? This too, should be considered an opportunity. Firstly, it makes transparent to the CAE that something needs to be improved. Secondly, this can be used for initiating improvements to the achievement of the customer value proposition. Thirdly, it provides the

CAE the possibility to assume the responsibility and accountability of the audit activities. Executive management and the board will appreciate transparency, even when that points to weaknesses in the audit function. As long as the CAE presents an improvement plan at the same time, it will not negatively affect her standing or reputation.

Impact on process owner

The process owner and lower management are only affected by this risk to the extent that it relates to support activities for which they believe that assurance is provided. When local management see daily activities of an auditor in their operations, they will first think that the auditor is performing audit assurance work. However, when the auditor is supporting the roll out of a new internal control system over financial reporting, or supporting the roll out of a new code of conduct, then local management will falsely think that they are going to receive audit assurance. Good upfront communication on the scope and content of work may avoid this risk.

Impact on division/business unit management

Division/business unit management will only be impacted in case they expect audit activity summaries for their business. In case they have no expectations (which is rather common), and they do not receive something, this risk is irrelevant to them. Still, similar to the above description of the opportunities, the CAE has an opportunity towards division/business unit management as well. In my personal experience, seizing such opportunities will increase the reputation and acceptability of the audit function with these senior business leaders. They will appreciate such information, even when they do not ask for it. Division/business unit management are equally affected as the process owner and lower management, in so far, the work of the auditor relates to support activities for which they believe that assurance is provided.

Impact on executive management and audit committee/board

To a large extent executive management and the board will leave it up to the CAE to determine the details and completeness of the reporting. They may have certain minimum requirements, but in my personal experience, these requirements are usually on the lower side of what can be delivered. They will probably not expect a balanced scorecard reporting or an annual report for the audit function, and may have no requirement for such information. Unless the information left out of the reporting is basic (and critical from their perspective), they will not claim for more reporting. For them less reporting is usually of more value than an overload of data.

Executive management and the board may not see such a reporting gap, but the CAE should be aware of this risk. As described before, the CAE should seize the reporting opportunities when they present themselves. The CAE can trigger these opportunities herself.

Insufficient reporting about the support and consulting work may lead the board and executive management to falsely believe that audit assurance was provided.

Risk drivers

The following risk drivers influence the level of risk of insufficient reporting on audit function activities, and the lower each of these elements, the higher the risk:

- The level of understanding the reporting requirements from the key customers.
- The experience, creativity and quality of the CAE.
- The clarity of communication on support and consulting work.

Determining risk levels

A high risk of insufficient reporting on the audit function activities may occur when: the CAE insufficiently communicates with the key customers; the reporting requirements of the key customers are not known; the CAE is inexperienced, or is not creative; best practice reporting is not followed.

A low risk of insufficient reporting on the audit function activities may occur when: the CAE is experienced and creative; best practice audit function reporting is applied; the CAE has a good understanding of the reporting requirements of the key customers; the CAE is frequently coordinating the content of reporting.

Audit Risk 6: Compliance Risks

Figure 38 – Eight Elements of Compliance Risk

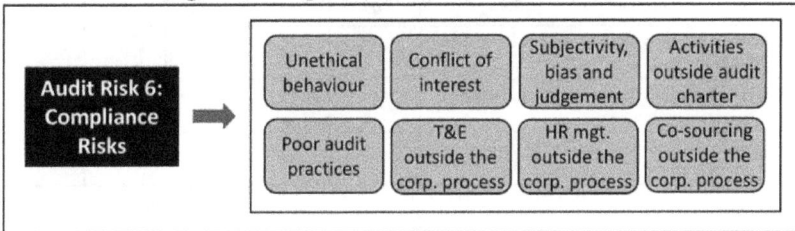

Audit Risk 6: Compliance Risks	Unethical behaviour	Conflict of interest	Subjectivity, bias and judgement	Activities outside audit charter
	Poor audit practices	T&E outside the corp. process	HR mgt. outside the corp. process	Co-sourcing outside the corp. process

The compliance risk is the risk that the audit activities conducted by the department and auditors are not compliant with the internal and external laws, regulations and policies. The board and management generally expect full compliance, and non-compliance will endanger the achievement of the customer value proposition.

In the following Compliance Risk Matrix, the eight compliance risks from the *Audit Risks Catalogue*© are matched with the five compliance objectives from the *Audit Objectives Catalogue*©. In the Compliance Risk Map, the eight compliance risks are mapped to the audit function's customer value proposition. The conclusions from this matrix and map are:

- The highest impact compliance risks for the audit function are the risks of poor audit practices and unethical behaviour.

- All eight risks apply to the audit function policies. This means that the main requirements for managing the compliance risks of the audit function can be captured in the audit function manual or handbook.

Figure 39 – Compliance Risk Matrix

COMPLIANCE RISK MATRIX					
Compliance Objectives: / Compliance Risks:	CO-1: Audit charter	CO-2: Audit policies	CO-3: Company policies	CO-4: IIA's IPPF	CO-5: IIA's code of ethics
CR-1: Unethical behaviour	✓	✓	✓	✓	✓
CR-2: Conflict of interest	✓	✓	✓	✓	✓
CR-3: Subjectivity, bias and judgement	✓	✓		✓	✓
CR-4: Activities outside the audit function's charter	✓	✓		✓	
CR-5: Poor audit practices	✓	✓		✓	
CR-6: Travel & Entertainment outside the corporate procedures		✓	✓		
CR-7: HR management of the auditors outside the corporate procedures		✓	✓		
CR-8: Engaging co-sourcing outside the corporate procedures		✓	✓		

Figure 40 – Compliance Risk Map

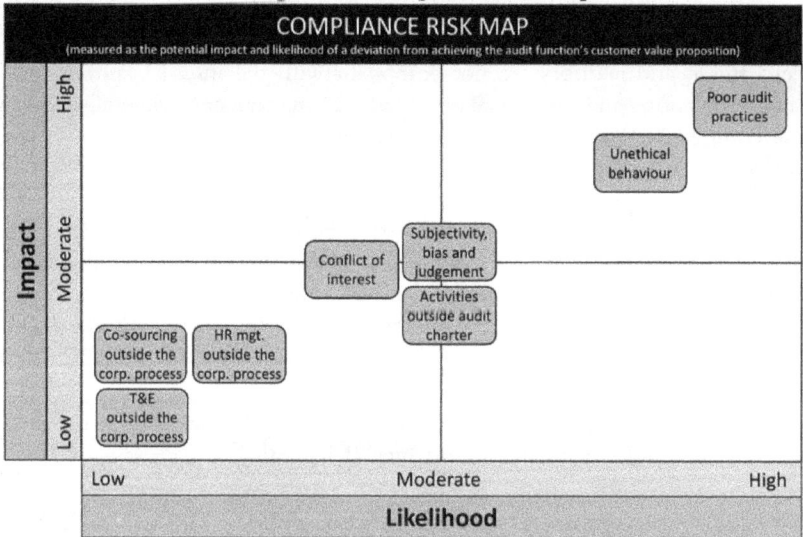

COMPLIANCE RISK MAP
(measured as the potential impact and likelihood of a deviation from achieving the audit function's customer value proposition)

The chapter is divided into three sections:
1. Risk of non-compliance with the audit charter and the audit function policies (CR-1 to 8)
2. Risk of non-compliance with The IIA's professional requirements (CR-1 to 5)
3. Risk of non-compliance with the company policies (CR-6 to 8)

Risk of non-compliance with audit charter and policies

Definition

The risk of non-compliance with the audit charter and the audit function policies is the probability that the audit activities do not adhere to the processes, procedures and requirements as laid down in the audit charter and the audit department policies.

Examples

An auditor performs a review of a subject matter for which he had the management responsibility till four months ago. An auditor does not prepare an audit planning document or does not document the results of his testing in the working papers. The CAE accepts an additional management role as head of group accounting, whereas at the same time his team is conducting regular financial audits on that department.

Causes

The causes for the non-compliance with the audit charter and the audit function policies can lie in the lack of knowledge, the lack of understanding, the lack of execution or the lack of supervision. New auditors may not be familiar with the policies yet, but those non-compliances should be mitigated through the onboarding process or the supervision by the CAE. Executive management or the board may request the CAE to take on a temporary or permanent role outside the scope of the audit charter, when they believe that the added value of such a role is higher than the audit engagements that are being conducted.

Impact on audit function

The quality of the audit function's processes and procedures will be significantly impaired in case of large deviations from the audit charter and the audit function policies. These requirements describe the obligatory practices, and non-compliance is principally not an option. The charter and policies set out the requirements for achieving the customer value proposition, so any deviation may lead to a shortfall in the achievement of the expected audit value.

Impact on process owner, division/business unit management

The auditee, process owner and lower management, division/business unit management will not be aware of the audit charter and the audit function policies, and as such, they will not be able to recognise any non-compliances. They will not care whether an audit planning document is prepared or working papers are maintained.

Impact on executive management and audit committee/board

Executive management and the board may not know the exact requirements of the audit charter and departmental policies, but based on their extensive business experience, they will understand the general principles for achieving the audit customer value proposition. Since they are the key customers formulating the customer expectations, they will have a good idea what it needs to fulfil those requirements. Though, in my personal experience, the chance is rather low that these business leaders will criticise deviations from the audit function policies when these have no interfaces outside the audit function (as they will simply not be aware of it). Non-compliances that have a larger impact outside the audit function will be easily recognisable for management, and their enquiry may trigger risk mitigation, assuming that the CAE picks up on their comments.

Risk drivers

The following risk drivers have a major influence on the level of the compliance risk, and the lower each of these elements, the higher the risk:
- The proficiency and experience of the auditor/audit manager/CAE.
- The quality of the audit supervision processes.
- The effectiveness of the quality assurance and improvement programme.
- The frequency of the (internal or external) quality assessments.

Determining risk levels

The audit function has a high risk of non-compliance with the audit charter and the audit function policies when: the CAE and auditors are inexperienced; supervision processes are weak or absent; there is no quality assurance and improvement programme in place; no periodic internal or external quality assessments are performed.

The audit function has a low risk of non-compliance with the audit charter and the audit function policies when: supervision and quality control processes are formalised and effective; qualified and experienced auditors conduct the audit; periodic quality assessments take place.

Risk of non-compliance with IIA requirements

Definition

The risk of non-compliance with the IIA requirements is the probability that the audit activities do not adhere to the processes, procedures and requirements as laid down in the IIA's IPPF and code of ethics.

Examples

The audit function uses the phrase "Conforms with the International Standards for the Professional Practice of Internal Auditing", without having a quality assurance and improvement programme in place. The CAE does not perform risk assessments in establishing the priorities of the annual audit plan. The audit work performed and the results are not consistently documented. The CAE does not review the working papers. The CAE has a conflict of interest with the subject matter of an audit, but he does not disclose this conflict. Audit opinions have a high level of subjectivity as the auditors give better audit ratings when the process owner has a specific gender. The audit opinions for one division are always a lot more negative than for another division, despite the facts being comparable.

Causes

The causes for the non-compliance with the IIA's professional requirements can lie in the lack of knowledge, the lack of understanding or the lack of execution of the IIA's mandatory professional practices. Such causes may arise when the CAE's position is assigned to a business manager who has no prior (internal) audit experience.

Impact on audit function

The quality of the audit function's processes and procedures will be significantly impaired in case of large deviations from the IIA's requirements. These requirements describe the best practices, thus the lower the non-compliance, the higher the quality of the audit function's processes, and the higher the likelihood of achieving the customer value proposition and added value.

Impact on process owner

The auditee, process owner and lower management will not be aware of the IIA's professional audit requirements for the audit function, and as such, they will not be able to recognise any poor audit practices. When they do identify such poor practices, it is likely that they will not say anything about it to the audit team. They might gossip with the other managers, but they will unlikely voice their concerns to the CAE.

In case the auditors show unethical behaviour, subjectivity, bias and judgement, or have a conflict of interest, the process owner will be impacted, as he will be directly affected through the audit engagement. Usually, the process owner will make himself heard by voicing his discontent with an unfair or biased treatment to the auditors and to the higher management levels. This communication should normally result in a mitigation of the relevant compliance risk.

Impact on division/business unit management

Division/business unit management's reaction will usually be the same as the process owner's response.

Impact on executive management and audit committee/board

Executive management and the board will have a general understanding of the good audit practices, and thus will be able to recognise a poor audit practice. It is unlikely that they know the exact requirements of the audit standards promulgated by the IIA, but based on their extensive business experience, they will understand the general principles that achieve quality in the audit processes and procedures. Executive management and the audit committee/board may identify poor audit practices based on complaints from the lower level managers or based on their own assessments through discussions with the CAE. In my personal experience, the chance is rather high that these business leaders will comment upon poor audit practices, when they see that these fall short of their general understanding of what good audit processes entail. As such, their enquiry may trigger risk mitigation.

Unethical behaviour will be considered as a significant issue by executive management and the audit committee/board. Since the audit function has a leading and exemplary role in showing the highest standards of conduct, any misconduct will be taken extremely seriously. Unethical behaviour will likely lead to dismissal of the person. At the same time, executive management and the audit committee/board will ask the CAE to strengthen his code of ethics and ensure that all team members follow the stipulations.

Subjectivity, bias and judgement during audit work will mostly be visible through the audit reports that these high-level managers and board members receive. If the lower level managers do not complain, they can only identify such behaviour based on the wording and conclusions in the audit reports. In case they receive all original audit reports, they may discover trends in the subjectivity, bias and judgements expressed through the wordings. For the reports with significant audit issues, they may question the CAE about the fairness and accuracy of the opinions and conclusions.

Risk drivers

The following risk drivers influence the level of the compliance risk, and the lower each of these elements, the higher the risk:

- The proficiency and experience of the auditor/audit manager/CAE.
- The quality of the audit supervision processes.
- The effectiveness of the quality assurance and improvement programme.
- The frequency of the (internal or external) quality assessments.

Determining risk levels

The audit function has a high risk of non-compliance with the IIA's IPPF and code of ethics when: the CAE and auditors are inexperienced; supervision processes are weak or absent; there is no quality assurance and improvement programme in place; no periodic internal or external quality assessments are performed; the CAE does not lead by showing exemplary ethical behaviour.

The audit function has a low risk of non-compliance with the IIA's IPPF and code of ethics when: supervision and quality control processes are formalised and effective; qualified and experienced auditors conduct the audit; periodic quality assessments take place; each year the audit team discusses and signs the code of ethics.

Risk of non-compliance with company policies

Definition

The risk of non-compliance with the company policies is the probability that the audit activities do not adhere to the company's policies, directives, processes, and procedures.

Examples

The compensation packages of the auditors do not comply with the company's remuneration practices and policies. Individual auditors frequently deviate from the corporate hotel booking policies. Audit co-sourcing decisions are based on the personal preferences of the CAE, without the formal tendering procedures to three service providers. The expense reports of the auditors do not require approval by the CAE before being paid out.

Causes

The causes for the non-compliance with the company policies can lie in the lack of knowledge, the lack of understanding or the lack of execution of the company policies and directives. Such causes may arise when the CAE or the auditors are new to the company.

Impact on audit function

The impact on achieving the customer value proposition may be negligible. However, the CAE will most likely be criticised for not following the corporate policies. Since the audit function must show exemplary behaviour, this could cause (not audit related) damage to the reputation of the audit function.

Impact on process owner, division/business unit management

It is unlikely that the auditee, process owner, lower management or division/business unit management's will be aware of the non-compliance with the company policies, as these are audit function internal processes interfacing with the corporate policies.

Impact on executive management and audit committee/board

Executive management will most likely be informed by the relevant corporate function about the non-compliance of the audit function. The board will usually not be informed, as long as the non-compliance is of a minor nature. Both will want the audit function to be fully compliant with the company policies, so as soon as they find out, they will request the CAE to take the corrective measures. In case the non-compliance is a blatant disregard of the corporate policies, this could have more severe repercussions for the CAE.

Risk drivers

The following risk drivers have a major influence on the level of the compliance risk, and the lower each of these elements, the higher the risk:

- The duration of employment of the auditor/audit manager/CAE.
- The quality of the approval procedures for the administrative processes in the audit function.

Determining risk levels

The audit function has a high risk of non-compliance with the company policies when: the CAE and auditors are new to the company; supervision processes over administrative procedures are weak or absent.

The audit function has a low risk of non-compliance with the company policies when: the CAE and auditors are long time employees; supervision processes over administrative procedures are strong; the CAE has a good understanding of the corporate policies and these are reflected in his audit handbook.

PART IV

-

AUDIT RISK MITIGATION

Figure 41 - PART IV: Audit Risk Mitigation

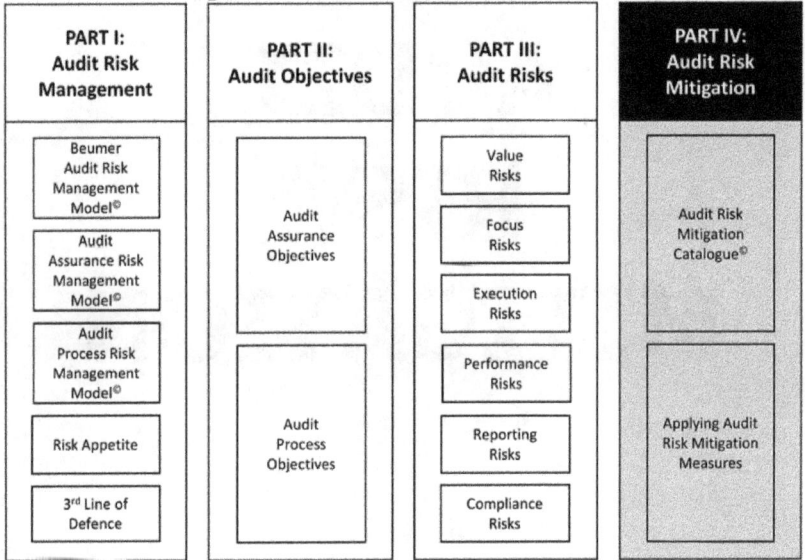

PART I: Audit Risk Management	PART II: Audit Objectives	PART III: Audit Risks	PART IV: Audit Risk Mitigation
Beumer Audit Risk Management Model©		Value Risks	
Audit Assurance Risk Management Model©	Audit Assurance Objectives	Focus Risks	Audit Risk Mitigation Catalogue©
Audit Process Risk Management Model©		Execution Risks	
Risk Appetite	Audit Process Objectives	Performance Risks	Applying Audit Risk Mitigation Measures
3rd Line of Defence		Reporting Risks	
		Compliance Risks	

Audit Risk Mitigation

Audit risk mitigation categories

Consistent with the *Beumer Audit Risk Management Model©*, the risk mitigation has the aim to reduce the gap between the targeted audit value and the expected audit value (whether measured quantitatively or qualitatively) to an acceptable level that is within the risk appetite of the board. Following the same structure as in the chapters *Audit Objectives* and *Audit Risks*, the following audit risk mitigations can be defined:

Strategy risk mitigations

Strategy risks mitigation: mitigation of the risk that the audit function strategic objectives are not achieved. Consistent with the strategy risks of value and focus, two risk mitigation categories can be defined:

Value risk mitigation: mitigating the risk that the activities of the audit function do not create added value to management and the board. Reducing this risk is all about gaining trust and credibility. It has a lot to do with the management of the CAE's personal relationships and communications with the leaders of the organisation. The following measures are suitable for reducing this risk:

- Improve the "connection" with management and the board
- Speak the language of management and the board
- Reduce the expectations gap
- Define a clear and focused audit charter
- Enhance the audit strategy and objectives to add value
- Develop and use marketing and promotional materials
- Increase the annual audit plan focus on the business topics of concern to management and the board
- Present the audit results in management and board meetings
- Focus the audit engagements on identifying significant issues
- Define efficient and cost-effective audit issue risk mitigating measures

- Actively manage the audit function productivity and performance
- Increase the leverage of audit cost

Focus risk mitigation: mitigating the risk that the activities of the audit function do not focus on the company's activities which are critical for management and the board to achieve their strategies and objectives. Reducing this risk is all about involving management and obtaining a good understanding of the business, their objectives and risk profile. It has a lot to do with information management. The following measures are suitable for reducing this risk:

- Increase the understanding of the business, company and subject matter
- Have a broad view on the business topics for which the audit function may be able to provide assurance
- Strengthen the risk assessment processes
- Increase the coordination with the process owner, management and the board
- Coordinate the audit work with the 2nd line of defence and the external auditors
- Improve the proficiency and experience of the auditor/audit manager/CAE
- Improve the access to critical data, information, transactions, projects, initiatives, and management
- Improve the completeness of the audit universe

Operations risk mitigations

Operations risk mitigation: mitigating the risk that the audit function processes and the use of the audit resources are not effective or efficient. Consistent with the operations risks of execution and performance, two risk mitigation categories can be defined:

Execution risk mitigation: mitigating the risk that the annual audit plan is not properly developed and implemented, or the audit engagements are not executed in a proper way, in achieving the customer value proposition. Reducing this risk is all about having the right processes in place to identify the significant issues. The risk of overlooking significant issues is the number one risk which the CAEs are always most cautious of. Therefore, the CAE must make sure that the audit accurately and completely identifies all the relevant issues in the subject matter, that these relevant issues are all sufficiently substantiated, and that the performed audit work is sufficient to meet the objectives of the audit. The following measures are suitable for reducing the execution risk:

- Timely audit announcements and appropriate audit scheduling
- Manage the short-term audit capacity shortfalls
- Improve the proficiency and experience of the auditor/audit manager/CAE
- Increase the quality and standardisation of the audit processes and procedures
- Improve the supervision and quality control processes
- Improve the focus of the work programme on the risk profile of the subject matter
- Increase the internal communication and feedback
- Improve the quality of the working paper documentation
- Brainstorm on the potential significant issues
- Increase the understanding of the business, company and subject matter
- Improve the access to critical data, information, transactions, projects, initiatives, and management
- Increase the coordination with the process owner, management and the board
- Think as management and the board
- Assess the subject matter and the audit results in the larger perspective
- Improve the appropriate risk mitigation measures for the identified risks
- Improve the process for identifying and handling scope limitations

Performance risk mitigation: mitigating the risk that the audit function processes and the use of the audit resources are not effective or efficient. Reducing this risk is all about managing the audit team's performance. It has a lot to do with productivity and efficiency in generating the output. The following measures are suitable for reducing this risk:

- Actively manage the audit function productivity and performance
- Utilise the performance management cycle
- Set clear deadlines
- Increase the standardisation of the audit processes
- Increase the automation of the audit processes
- Make the costs of the audit activities transparent
- Increase the leverage of the audit cost
- Improve the proficiency and experience of the auditor/audit manager/CAE
- Better structure and organise the audit work and planning
- Improve the supervision and quality control processes

- Increase the internal communication and feedback

Reporting risk mitigations

Reporting risk mitigation: mitigating the risk that the audit reporting does not accurately and completely reflect the audit function's activities and the achievement of the customer value proposition. Reducing this risk is all about transmitting clear messages to the right managers. At the audit function level this relates to reporting to executive management and the audit committee; at the audit engagement level this relates to the audit engagement reports. The following measures are suitable for reducing this risk:

- Increase the understanding of the reporting requirements from the key customers
- Clear communications about the differences between audit assurance and support/consulting work
- Critically review the completeness of the audit report distribution lists
- Benchmark the audit function reporting against the best practices
- Increase the standardisation of the reporting requirements and processes
- Improve the proficiency and experience of the auditor/audit manager/CAE
- Train the auditors in writing business-like audit reports
- Improve the supervision and quality control processes
- Improve the facts, quantifications and storyline in the reports

Compliance risk mitigations

Compliance risk mitigation: mitigating the risk that the audit activities conducted by the department and auditors are not compliant with the internal and external laws, regulations and policies. Reducing this risk is all about following the relevant regulations and policies. The board and management generally expect full compliance, and non-compliance will endanger the achievement of the customer value proposition. The following measures are suitable for reducing this risk:

- Train the audit team on the content of the audit charter and the audit function policies
- Improve the proficiency and experience of the auditor/audit manager/CAE
- Set up a professional development programme for each auditor
- Train the auditors on the IIA's IPPF requirements

- Discuss and sign the code of ethics
- Improve the supervision and quality control processes
- Maintain an effective quality assurance and improvement programme
- Regularly perform the internal quality self-assessments and periodically engage an external assessor
- Training on the company policies and administrative procedures
- Clear approval procedures

Audit Risk Mitigation Catalogue©

The *Audit Risk Mitigation Catalogue©* in Table 3 can be used as a checklist for mitigating the audit risks. The risk mitigation measures are further detailed and explained in the next chapters.

Audit risk mitigations overlapping between categories

Ten measures occur in multiple mitigation categories:

- Improve auditor proficiency/experience: occurs in focus risk mitigation (FRM-6), execution risk mitigation (ERM-3), performance risk mitigation (PRM-8), reporting risk mitigation (RRM-6), and compliance risk mitigation (CRM-2).

- Improve supervision and quality control: occurs in execution risk mitigation (ERM-5), performance risk mitigation (PRM-10), reporting risk mitigation (RRM-8) and compliance risk mitigation (CRM-6).

- Increase understanding of the business and company: occurs in focus risk mitigation (FRM-1) and execution risk mitigation (ERM-10).

- Improve access to information: occurs in focus risk mitigation (FRM-7) and execution risk mitigation (ERM-11).

- Increase coordination with the board/management: occurs in focus risk mitigation (FRM-4) and execution risk mitigation (ERM-12).

- Improve the efficiency and effectiveness of the audit issue risk mitigating measures: occurs in value risk mitigation (VRM-10) and execution risk mitigation (ERM-15).

- Increase internal communication and feedback: occurs in execution risk mitigation (ERM-7) and performance risk mitigation (PRM-11).

- Improve productivity management: occurs in value risk mitigation (VRM-11) and performance risk mitigation (PRM-1).

- Increase audit cost leverage: occurs in value risk mitigation (VRM-12) and performance risk mitigation (PRM-7).

- Improve process standardisation: occurs in execution risk mitigation (ERM-4) and performance risk mitigation (PRM-4).

When the double counts are eliminated, the net number of audit risk mitigations amounts to 51.

The fact that 10 measures occur in multiple mitigation categories leads to the following conclusions:

- Improving the auditor/audit manager/CAE proficiency and experience, together with strengthening the supervision and quality control, are the biggest levers for mitigating the audit risks. These two measures address the risks in five categories.
  Hiring more experienced auditors, training and developing the auditors, combined with a closer supervision of the critical audit work will strongly mitigate the risks in the focus, execution, performance, reporting and compliance categories, and therefore also contribute to the value risk mitigation.

- Better understanding of the business and company, better access to critical information and improved coordination with management and the board are all intertwined mitigations. They will result in an improved focus and a better execution.

Table 3 – Audit Risk Mitigation Catalogue©

Audit Assurance Risk Mitigation	
1. Value Risk Mitigation	
VRM-1	Improve the "connection" with management and the board
VRM-2	Speak the language of management and the board
VRM-3	Reduce the expectations gap
VRM-4	Define a clear and focused audit charter
VRM-5	Enhance the audit strategy and objectives to add value
VRM-6	Develop and use marketing and promotional materials
VRM-7	Increase audit plan focus on business topics of concern to management and the board
VRM-8	Present audit results in management and board meetings
VRM-9	Focus audit engagements on identifying significant issues
VRM-10	Define efficient and cost-effective audit issue risk mitigating measures
VRM-11	Actively manage audit function productivity and performance
VRM-12	Increase leverage of audit cost
2. Focus Risk Mitigation	
FRM-1	Increase understanding of the business, company and subject matter
FRM-2	Have a broad view on the business topics for which the audit function may be able to provide assurance
FRM-3	Strengthen the risk assessment process
FRM-4	Increase coordination with process owner, management and the board
FRM-5	Coordinate audit work with the 2nd line of defence and the external auditors
FRM-6	Improve proficiency and experience of auditor/audit manager/CAE
FRM-7	Improve access to critical data, information, transactions, projects, initiatives, and management
FRM-8	Improve completeness of the audit universe
3. Execution Risk Mitigation	
ERM-1	Timely audit announcements and appropriate scheduling
ERM-2	Manage short-term audit capacity shortfalls
ERM-3	Improve proficiency and experience of auditor/audit manager/CAE
ERM-4	Increase quality and standardisation of audit processes and procedures
ERM-5	Improve supervision and quality control processes
ERM-6	Improve the focus of the work programme on the risk profile of subject matter
ERM-7	Increase internal communication and feedback
ERM-8	Improve quality of working paper documentation
ERM-9	Brainstorm on potential significant issues

ERM-10	Increase understanding of the business, company and subject matter
ERM-11	Improve access to critical data, information, transactions, projects, initiatives, and management
ERM-12	Increase coordination with process owner, management and the board
ERM-13	Think as management and the board
ERM-14	Assess subject matter and audit results in the larger perspective
ERM-15	Improve appropriate risk mitigation measures for identified risks
ERM-16	Improve process for identifying and handling scope limitations
Audit Process Risk Mitigation	
4. Performance Risk Mitigation	
PRM-1	Actively manage audit function productivity and performance
PRM-2	Utilise performance management cycle
PRM-3	Set clear deadlines
PRM-4	Increase quality and standardisation of audit processes and procedures
PRM-5	Increase automation of audit processes
PRM-6	Make costs of audit activities transparent
PRM-7	Increase leverage of audit cost
PRM-8	Improve proficiency and experience of auditor/audit manager/CAE
PRM-9	Better structure and organise audit work and planning
PRM-10	Improve supervision and quality control processes
PRM-11	Increase internal communication and feedback
5. Reporting Risk Mitigation	
RRM-1	Increase understanding of reporting requirements from key customers
RRM-2	Clear communications about differences between assurance and support/consulting
RRM-3	Critically review completeness of audit report distribution list
RRM-4	Benchmark audit function reporting against best practices
RRM-5	Increase standardisation of reporting requirements and processes
RRM-6	Improve proficiency and experience of auditor/audit manager/CAE
RRM-7	Train auditors in writing business-like audit reports
RRM-8	Improve supervision and quality control processes
RRM-9	Improve facts, quantifications and storyline
6. Compliance Risk Mitigation	
CRM-1	Train audit team on content of audit charter and audit function policies
CRM-2	Improve proficiency and experience of auditor/audit manager/CAE

CRM-3	Set up professional development programme for each auditor
CRM-4	Train auditors on IIA's IPPF requirements
CRM-5	Discuss and sign code of ethics
CRM-6	Improve supervision and quality control processes
CRM-7	Maintain effective quality assurance and improvement programme
CRM-8	Regularly perform internal quality self-assessments and periodically engage external assessor
CRM-9	Training on company policies and administrative procedures
CRM-10	Clear approval procedures

Audit Assurance Risk Mitigation

Figure 42 – Three Audit Assurance Risk Mitigation Categories

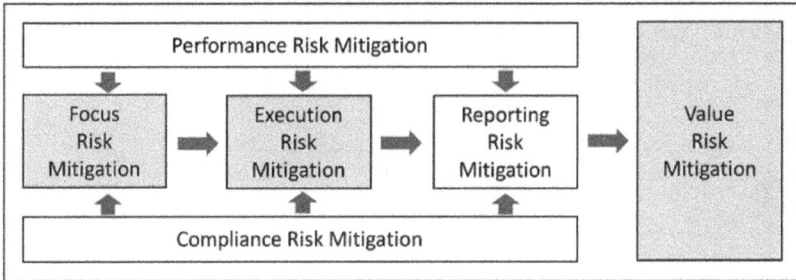

Performance Risk Mitigation			
Focus Risk Mitigation	Execution Risk Mitigation	Reporting Risk Mitigation	Value Risk Mitigation
Compliance Risk Mitigation			

In the next three chapters, each of the three audit assurance risk mitigation categories (value risk mitigation, focus risk mitigation and execution risk mitigation), together with the 36 risk mitigation measures from the *Audit Risk Mitigation Catalogue©*, are described and analysed in detail. The chapters have the following structure:

- A risk mitigation matrix matches the risks from the *Audit Risk Mitigation Catalogue©* with the risk categories, consistent with the *Audit Assurance Risk Mitigation Tree©*.

- Each of the individual risk mitigation measures is described and analysed in detail. Since the majority of the individual risk mitigation measures address multiple risk subcategories, only the first subchapter for which a risk mitigation measure is applicable an elaborate explanation will be provided. In the following subchapters that repeat these mitigation measures, only the titles of these measures are listed.

Audit Assurance Risk Mitigation Tree©

The *Audit Assurance Risk Mitigation Tree©* captures all 36 mitigation measures in one chart.

Figure 43 – Audit Assurance Risk Mitigation Tree©

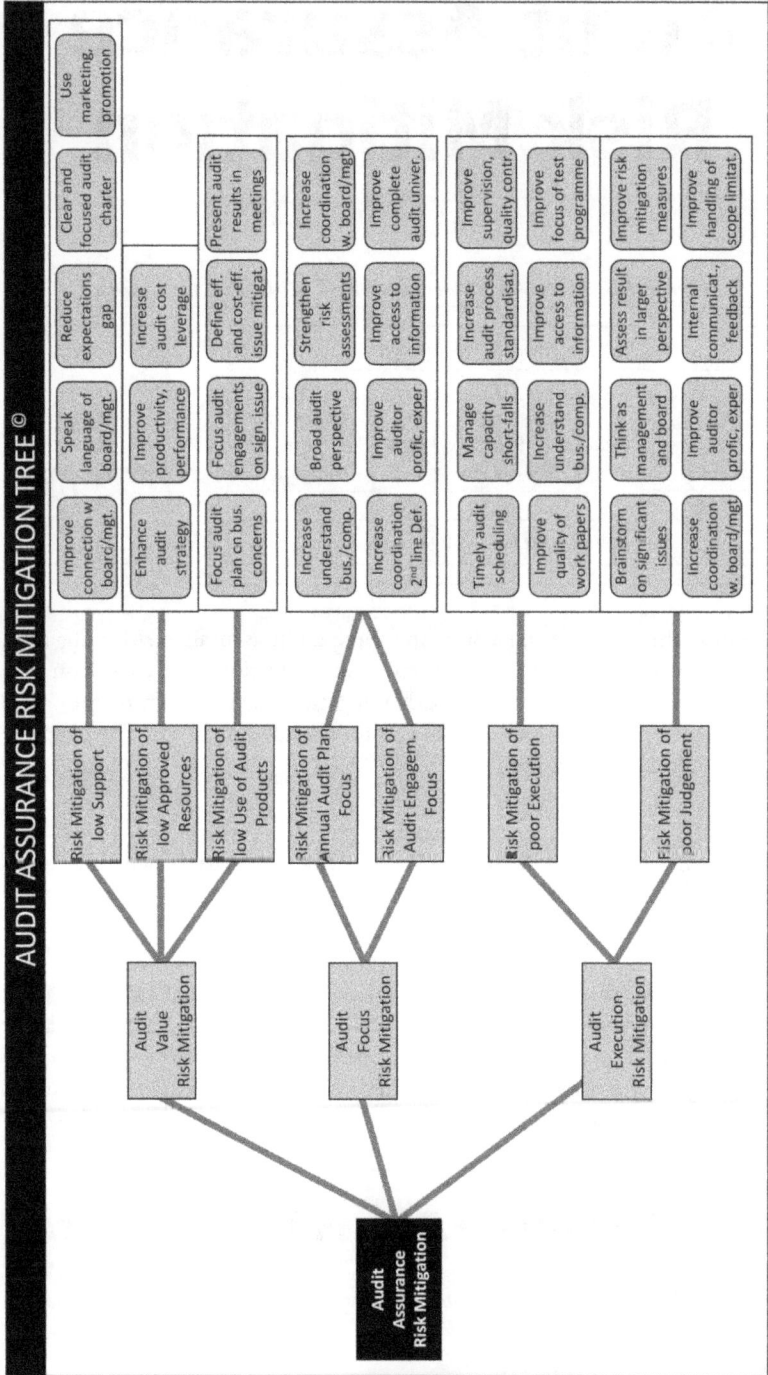

Audit Risk Mitigation 1: Value Risk Mitigation

Figure 44 – Twelve Elements of Value Risk Mitigation

Audit Risk Mitigation 1: Value Risk Mitigation				
	Improve connection w board/mgt.	Speak language of board/mgt.	Reduce expectations gap	Clear and focused audit charter
	Enhance audit strategy	Use marketing, promotion	Focus audit plan on bus. concerns	Present audit results in meetings
	Focus audit engagements on sign. issue	Define eff. and cost-eff. issue mitigat.	Improve productivity, performance	Increase audit cost leverage

Value risk mitigation is mitigating the risk that the activities of the audit function do not create added value to management and the board.

In the following Value Risk Mitigation Matrix, the 12 value risk mitigation measures from the *Audit Risk Mitigation Catalogue*© are matched with the three value risk categories, consistent with the *Audit Assurance Risk Mitigation Tree*©. The conclusions from this matrix are:

- Most of the measures have an equally important contribution to the mitigation of the value risk. This means that there is not one specific measure, but rather the combination of several measures, that reduce the value risk.

- As already mentioned in earlier chapters, the value risk is often a result of the focus and execution risks. Therefore, mitigating these two risks will provide a significant contribution to mitigating the value risk as well.

Figure 45 – Value Risk Mitigation Matrix

VALUE RISK MITIGATION MATRIX			
Value Risk Categories: / Value Risk Mitigation:	Risk mitigation of low support	Risk mitigation of low approved resources	Risk mitigation of low use of audit products
VRM-1: Improve the "connection" with management and the board	✓	✓	✓
VRM-2: Speak the language of management and the board	✓	✓	✓
VRM-3: Reduce the expectations gap	✓	✓	✓
VRM-4: Define a clear and focused audit charter	✓		
VRM-5: Enhance the audit strategy and objectives to add value	✓	✓	✓
VRM-6: Develop and use marketing and promotional materials	✓	✓	✓
VRM-7: Increase audit plan focus on business topics of concern to management and the board	✓	✓	✓
VRM-8: Present audit results in management and board meetings			✓
VRM-9: Focus audit engagements on identifying significant issues	✓	✓	✓
VRM-10: Define efficient and cost-effective audit issue risk mitigating measures			✓
VRM-11: Actively manage audit function productivity and performance	✓	✓	
VRM-12: Increase leverage of audit cost		✓	

The chapter is divided into three sections:
1. Risk mitigation of low support (VRM-1 to 7, VRM-9, VRM-11)
2. Risk mitigation of low approved resources (VRM-1 to 3, VRM-5 to 7, VRM-9, VRM-11 to 12)
3. Risk mitigation of low use of the audit products (VRM-1 to 3, VRM-5 to 10)

Risk mitigation of low support

VRM-1: Improve the "connection" with management and the board
Improve the way the CAE "connects" with the process owner, management and the board, and improve the quality of the relationships. Embark on a "tour" to establish rapport and build personal relationships. Study what drives management and learn their business and speak their language. Single out the individual managers who have an acceptance problem. Target them to build better relationships and convince them of the added value of the audit function.

VRM-2: Speak the language of management and the board
The board and management talk about strategies, achieving objectives, implementing initiatives, organisational structures, business models, product life cycles, financial statements, regulatory requirements, business

operations, management tools, ERP systems, reporting systems, incentive schemes, culture and ethics, and so forth. If the CAE speaks the same language, and is able to have business discussions with management and the board, she will gain trust and credibility.

This risk mitigation measure corresponds to the chapter *Understanding the Company and Business*, as described in *Volume I* of *Driving Audit Value*.

VRM-3: Reduce the expectations gap

Increase the goal-congruence between the focus of the audit function and the focus of the process owner, management and the board. Identify the causes for the expectations gap, and reduce the gap by targeted activities.

This risk mitigation measure corresponds to the chapter *Audit Value*, as described in *Volume I* of *Driving Audit Value*, particularly the subchapter titled *managing customer expectations*.

VRM-4: Define a clear and focused audit charter

Ensure that the audit charter focuses on adding audit value and uses all the right wording to provide the support for the execution of the audit strategy. Have the audit charter approved by the board and executive management. A clear and approved audit charter can serve as guidance for the expectations and added value. This can be used as a communication tool to manage the expectations of management.

This risk mitigation measure corresponds to the chapter *Internal Audit Charter*, as described in *Volume I* of *Driving Audit Value*.

VRM-5: Enhance the audit strategy and objectives to add value

Redefine the audit strategy and objectives to ensure that they are focused on providing maximum added value to the board and management. Monitor the effective and efficient implementation of the audit function's strategy and objectives. Define a clear added value strategy. Redefine the customer value proposition through discussions with the board and executive management.

This risk mitigation measure corresponds to the chapter *Audit Value*, as described in *Volume I* of *Driving Audit Value*.

VRM-6: Develop and use marketing and promotional materials

Develop and use marketing and promotional materials. Promote the principles of good governance and the added value role of the audit function. Share success stories and have supportive managers spread the positive word. Make sure that all management levels understand the strategy to maximise the added value of the audit function.

VRM-7: **Increase audit plan focus on business topics of concern to management and the board**

Convince management of the role and benefit of the audit function by having the right focus in the annual audit plan on those business topics which are of concern to management and the board.

This risk mitigation measure corresponds to the chapter *Annual Audit Plan*, as described in *Volume I* of *Driving Audit Value*, as well as to the next chapter.

VRM-9: **Focus audit engagements on identifying significant issues**

Focus the audit engagements on identifying the significant audit issues. Capture the interest of the process owner, management and the board with interesting and added value audit issues.

This risk mitigation measure corresponds to *Volume III* of *Driving Audit Value: Audit Engagement Strategy*.

VRM-11: **Actively manage audit function productivity and performance**

Actively manage the productivity, efficiency and effectiveness of the audit function. Increase the focus of the quality assurance and improvement programme to ensure that the audit results that are presented in the audit reports make interesting and high quality reading. Ensure that the audit reports are short and concise, with clear wording and messages. Use good business English, present relevant data, draw the right conclusions, and present the topics in an orderly way. Increase the number and quality of audit reports produced.

This risk mitigation measure corresponds to the chapter *Performance Management*, as described in *Volume I* of *Driving Audit Value*, as well as to the chapter *Performance Risk Mitigation* in this book.

Risk mitigation of low approved resources

VRM-1: Improve the "connection" with management and the board
VRM-2: Speak the language of management and the board
VRM-3: Reduce the expectations gap
VRM-5: Enhance the audit strategy and objectives to add value
VRM-6: Develop and use marketing and promotional materials
VRM-7: Increase audit plan focus on business topics of concern to management and the board
VRM-9: Focus audit engagements on identifying significant issues

VRM-11: Actively manage audit function productivity and performance

VRM-12: Increase leverage of audit cost

Leverage the audit cost so that the average cost per audit day is far below the comparable costs of outsourcing. Lower the costs of the individual audit projects. Increase the use of automation, improve the efficiency of the audit work programme steps and testing methodology, leverage the audit teams, critically assess the duration of the audits (try to shorten) as well as the number of auditors (try to reduce) on one assignment, reassess the extensiveness of the working paper documentation requirements, introduce workflow management and standardise the processes. Use exception reporting for the audit reports, instead of full descriptions of all audit work, and reduce the number of pages in the audit report by reshaping style, format and content.

This risk mitigation measure corresponds to the chapter *Performance Management*, as described in *Volume I* of *Driving Audit Value*, as well as to the chapter *Performance Risk Mitigation* in this book.

Risk mitigation of low use of the audit products

VRM-1: Improve the "connection" with management and the board
VRM-2: Speak the language of management and the board
VRM-3: Reduce the expectations gap
VRM-5: Enhance the audit strategy and objectives to add value
VRM-6: Develop and use marketing and promotional materials
VRM-7: Increase audit plan focus on business topics of concern to management and the board

VRM-8: Present audit results in management and board meetings

Put the discussion of the audit results on the agenda of the executive management meetings and the audit committee meetings. Assuming that the CAE can present audit results that are of interest to the board and executive management, do not only send them the reports, but also set up meetings to present those audit results. Such meetings will increase the positive attention to the audit added value, improve the visibility of the CAE, give the CAE the opportunity to understand the way of thinking of these business leaders, and enable a personal discussion on the topics brought forward.

VRM-9: Focus audit engagements on identifying significant issues

VRM-10: Define efficient and cost-effective audit issue risk mitigating measures

Ensure that the recommended audit issue risk mitigating measures are efficient, effective and have a low cost of implementation and maintenance.

This risk mitigation measure corresponds to the descriptions in *Volume III* of *Driving Audit Value*.

Audit Risk Mitigation 2: Focus Risk Mitigation

Figure 46 – Eight Elements of Focus Risk Mitigation

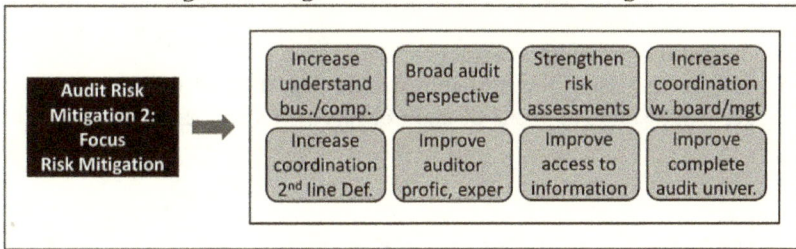

Audit Risk Mitigation 2: Focus Risk Mitigation	Increase understand bus./comp.	Broad audit perspective	Strengthen risk assessments	Increase coordination w. board/mgt
	Increase coordination 2nd line Def.	Improve auditor profic, exper	Improve access to information	Improve complete audit univer.

Focus risk mitigation is mitigating the risk that the activities of the audit function do not focus on the company's activities which are critical to management and the board for achieving their strategies and objectives.

In the following Focus Risk Mitigation Matrix, the eight focus risk mitigation measures from the *Audit Risk Mitigation Catalogue©* are matched with the two focus risk categories, consistent with the *Audit Assurance Risk Mitigation Tree©*. The conclusions from this matrix are:

- The focus risk mitigation is driven by a better understanding of the company and business, a stronger risk assessment process and increased coordination.

- As in the mitigation of all the risk categories, having proficient and experienced auditors is the basis for all improvement.

Figure 47 – Focus Risk Mitigation Matrix

FOCUS RISK MITIGATION MATRIX		
Focus Risk Categories: / Focus Risk Mitigation:	Risks of focus of annual audit plan	Risks of focus of audit engagements
FRM-1: Increase understanding of the business, company and subject matter	✓	✓
FRM-2: Have a broad view on the business topics for which the audit function may be able to provide assurance	✓	
FRM-3: Strengthen the risk assessment process	✓	✓
FRM-4: Increase coordination with process owner, management and the board	✓	✓
FRM-5: Coordinate audit work with the 2nd line of defence and external auditors	✓	✓
FRM-6: Improve proficiency and experience of auditor/audit manager/CAE	✓	✓
FRM-7: Improve access to critical data, information, transactions, projects, initiatives, and management	✓	✓
FRM-8: Improve completeness of the audit universe	✓	

The chapter is divided into two sections:
1. Risk mitigation of focus of annual audit plan (FRM-1 to 8)
2. Risk mitigation of focus of audit engagements (FRM-1 and FRM-3 to 7)

Risk mitigation of focus of annual audit plan

FRM-1: Increase understanding of the business, company and subject matter

This risk mitigation measure corresponds to the chapter *Understanding the Business and Company*, as described in *Volume I* of *Driving Audit Value*. This understanding has several aspects and applications:

General

The CAE and the people working for him must have a good understanding of the company. The CAE needs to go out in the field and talk to management to learn the business. He should review available business documents, process flows, KPIs, balanced scorecards, and financial information. The CAE should send the team to training courses for understanding the business, and learning how to audit specific processes. Ask the business managers to explain their operations and processes.

For the annual audit plan
Obtain and analyse all relevant information, which can give clues as to the topics that should be included in the audit universe. Review strategic business plans, budgets, lists of companies included and excluded from the consolidation, major project initiatives, corporate announcements, division/business unit announcements, and discuss the business developments, structure changes, and major projects with management at the division and corporate level. Only then can the CAE start putting together the annual audit plan. Alternatively, he may hire specialists and experts from outside the company to assist in putting together the right focus of the annual plan.

For the audit engagement
The auditors, the audit manager and CAE must have a good understanding of the subject matter. They must be trained and have prior experience in dealing with the topic. Alternatively, co-source or outsource the audit project, and hire a specialist and a well-experienced auditor from outside the company to perform the audit. Will a treasury audit of derivatives trading and positions be performed? Send the audit team to a training course to understand the topic, learn how to audit treasury processes, and then let the treasury department give an explanation of what they do. Only then start putting together the work programmes.

For the CAE to take responsibility
Even when the CAE co-sources or outsources, as long as the audit report is issued by his audit function, in his name, he must still understand the subject matter, despite its complexity. Co-sourcing or outsourcing does not relieve the CAE from his obligation in having a thorough understanding of the subject matter, the audit approach, the work performed, the audit results and their interpretation. He is still accountable for the product. The only way out of this is to completely outsource the audit, and let the outsourcer issue the report in their own name. But even then, the CAE needs to have a good understanding of the results, since the audit committee and executive management will ask him to explain this audit result. So, either way, he must be involved and understand the subject matter.

FRM-2: Have a broad view on the business topics for which the audit function may be able to provide assurance

Have a broad view on the business topics for which the audit function may be able to provide assurance. Consider strategy-related audit work. Do not limit the focus to low level control and compliance systems only.

This risk mitigation measure corresponds to the chapter *Annual Audit Plan*, as described in *Volume I* of *Driving Audit Value*. Particularly, have a look at the special topic: *why it matters to perform strategy-related audit work*.

FRM-3: Strengthen the risk assessment process

Strengthen the risk assessment process, improve the quality of the analysis of the risks and the business objectives. Identify the emerging risks and include them in the audit plan.

This risk mitigation measure corresponds to the chapter *Annual Audit Plan*, as described in *Volume I* of *Driving Audit Value*. Particularly, have a look at the subchapter *risk assessments*.

FRM-4: Increase coordination with process owner, management and the board

Increase the level of input by and coordination with the process owner, management and the board. At the start of the planning process inform executive management and the board how value will be added. Make sure that the audit planning and audit engagement preparations address the concerns of the board and management. Involve a broad range of management and the board, in discussing and setting priorities, at an early stage and a later confirmation stage during the annual audit planning process. Consult with the leading managers about the recent and upcoming business developments and their priorities. The more complex the company, the more unclear the strategies and business objectives, the more the CAE will need to communicate and coordinate.

This risk mitigation measure corresponds to the chapter *Coordination*, as described in *Volume I* of *Driving Audit Value*.

FRM-5: Coordinate audit work with the 2nd line of defence and external auditors

Coordinate audit work with the 2nd line of defence: management's risk mitigation functions such as compliance, risk reporting, legal, and group reporting. Understand their views on the company's emerging risk profile for the annual audit planning as well as for the audit engagements. Coordinate the audit assurance over the financial reporting with the external auditors. Identify any potential assurance duplications or gaps.

This risk mitigation measure corresponds to the chapter *Coordination*, as described in *Volume I* of *Driving Audit Value*.

FRM-6: Improve proficiency and experience of auditor/audit manager/CAE

Enhance the auditor's proficiency and experience with annual audit planning and audit engagement planning. The CAE must be able to handle the complexities, uncertainties and the highly dynamic business and management. He needs to understand the inherent risks and have the awareness how to mitigate their impact. Training of the auditors in the profession of internal audit (e.g. the CIA certification from The IIA) and training of the auditors in the audit function's internal procedures and processes (e.g. the working paper documentation requirements) to increase their level of proficiency.

FRM-7: Improve access to critical data, information, transactions, projects, initiatives, and management
Ensure access to all the information required. Convince executive management and the board of the need to access business information and the added value role of the audit function.

FRM-8: Improve completeness of the audit universe
Improve the completeness of the audit universe as well as the risk universe based on the access to critical information in determining the audit plan priorities.
This risk mitigation measure corresponds to the chapter *Annual Audit Plan*, as described in *Volume I* of *Driving Audit Value*. Particularly, have a look at the subchapter *audit universe*.

Risk mitigation of focus of audit engagements

FRM-1: Increase understanding of the business, company and subject matter
FRM-3: Strengthen the risk assessment process
FRM-4   Increase coordination with process owner, management and the board
FRM-5: Coordinate audit work with the 2nd line of defence and external auditors
FRM-6: Improve proficiency and experience of auditor/audit manager/CAE
FRM-7: Improve access to critical data, information, transactions, projects, initiatives, and management

Audit Risk Mitigation 3: Execution Risk Mitigation

Figure 48 – Sixteen Elements of Execution Risk Mitigation

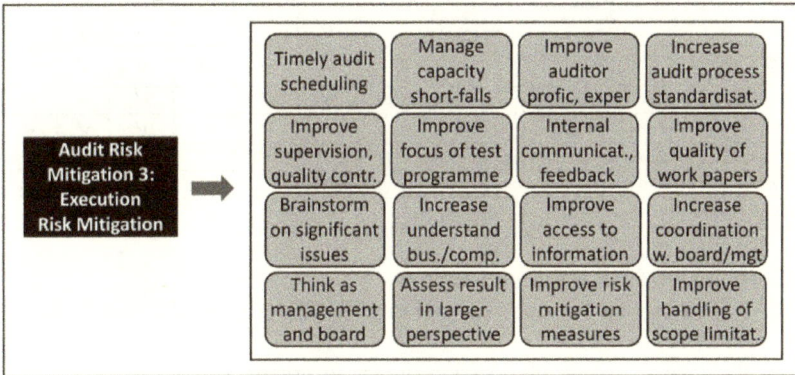

Timely audit scheduling	Manage capacity short-falls	Improve auditor profic, exper	Increase audit process standardisat.
Improve supervision, quality contr.	Improve focus of test programme	Internal communicat., feedback	Improve quality of work papers
Brainstorm on significant issues	Increase understand bus./comp.	Improve access to information	Increase coordination w. board/mgt
Think as management and board	Assess result in larger perspective	Improve risk mitigation measures	Improve handling of scope limitat.

(Audit Risk Mitigation 3: Execution Risk Mitigation →)

Execution risk mitigation is mitigating the risk that the annual audit plan is not properly developed and implemented, or the audit engagements are not executed in a proper way, for achieving the customer value proposition.

In the following Execution Risk Mitigation Matrix, the 16 execution risk mitigation measures from the *Audit Risk Mitigation Catalogue*© are matched with the six execution risk categories, consistent with the categorisation of the main execution risks as described in the chapter *Audit Risk 3: Execution Risks*. The conclusions from this matrix are:

- The execution risk and its mitigation is the largest category of all the risk mitigations, as the audit function can be exposed to six main types of execution risks, particularly in the audit engagements.

- As each CAE knows, the most important risk mitigation in the audit engagements relates to overlooking significant issues. The measures listed below provide guidance on how to overcome this risk.

Figure 49 – Execution Risk Mitigation Matrix

EXECUTION RISK MITIGATION MATRIX						
Execution Risk Categories: *Execution Risk Mitigation:*	Risk of poor execution	Risk of over-looking significant issues	Risk of agreeing no or wrong audit issue risk mitigation	Risk of wrong audit engage-ment conclu-sions	Risk of over-valuing small issues	Risk of over-looking scope limita-tions
ERM-1: Timely audit announcements and appropriate scheduling	✓					✓
ERM-2: Manage short-term audit capacity shortfalls	✓					✓
ERM-3: Improve proficiency and experience of auditor/audit manager/CAE	✓	✓	✓	✓	✓	✓
ERM-4: Increase quality and standardisation of audit processes and procedures	✓	✓	✓	✓	✓	✓
ERM-5: Improve supervision and quality control processes	✓	✓	✓	✓	✓	✓
ERM-6: Improve focus of work programme to risk profile of subject matter		✓		✓		✓
ERM-7: Increase internal communication and feedback	✓	✓	✓	✓	✓	✓
ERM-8: Improve quality of working paper documentation	✓	✓	✓	✓	✓	✓
ERM-9: Brainstorm on potential significant issues		✓		✓		
ERM-10: Increase understanding of the business, company and subject matter	✓	✓	✓	✓	✓	✓
ERM-11: Improve access to critical data, information, transactions, projects, initiatives, and management	✓	✓	✓	✓	✓	✓
ERM-12: Increase coordination with process owner, management and the board	✓	✓	✓	✓	✓	✓
ERM-13: Think as management and the board		✓	✓	✓	✓	✓
ERM-14: Assess subject matter and audit results in the larger perspective		✓	✓	✓	✓	
ERM-15: Improve appropriate risk mitigation measures for identified risks			✓			
ERM-16: Improve process for identifying and handling scope limitations						✓

The chapter is divided into six sections:

1. Risk mitigation of poor execution (ERM-1 to 5, ERM-7 and 8, ERM-10 to 12)
2. Risk mitigation of overlooking significant issues (ERM-3 to 14)
3. Risk mitigation of agreeing no or wrong audit issue risk mitigation measures (ERM-3 to 5, ERM-7 and 8, ERM-10 to 15)
4. Risk mitigation of wrong audit engagement conclusions (ERM-3 to 14)
5. Risk mitigation of over-valuing small issues (ERM-3 to 5, ERM-7 to 14)
6. Risk mitigation of overlooking scope limitations (ERM-1 to 8, ERM-10 to 14, ERM-16)

Most risk mitigation measures correspond to the topics as described in *Volume III* of *Driving Audit Value: Audit Engagement Strategy*. Reference is made to that book for more details.

Risk mitigation of poor execution

ERM-1: Timely audit announcements and appropriate scheduling
Eliminate potential scope limitations by making timely audit announcements, ensuring the full access to the subject matter information and people, and an appropriate time scheduling avoiding a collision with time-availability of the key auditees and process owners.

ERM-2: Manage short-term audit capacity shortfalls
Manage short-term audit capacity shortfalls by resetting the priorities and the scope for the audit engagements that are impacted by the reduction in (quantity or quality) of the audit resources. Consider whether co-sourcing may resolve a short-term capacity shortfall, reshuffle the timing of the audit projects or refocus the remaining audit resources from the lower priority to the higher priority audit engagements.

ERM-3: Improve proficiency and experience of auditor/audit manager/CAE
Increase the proficiency and development of the auditors, work with experienced auditors whose skills are further developed. Increase the quality of the auditor/audit manager/CAE through training, certifications and professional development. Improving the auditor's quality of judgement plays a particularly important role in the identification of the audit issues and the assessment of their significance. The auditor is on the front line, and it will often depend on his assessment whether a topic is raised as an audit issue, to what extent it is described in the audit working papers, and what attention he wants to give it for the achievement of the audit engagement objectives. The better this judgement, the lower the risk of overlooking significant issues.

In an environment with a high inherent risk, a checklist auditor would not be very useful. The CAE needs to have audit staff who can handle ambiguity, uncertainties, judgement, who are flexible, can think across the business models, and can work without overly structured and standardised audit processes. Do not use a check-list auditor who still needs to develop his/her judgement skills, unless the CAE has the resources to perform a close supervision. In the subject matter areas with a high degree of judgement, there is no right or wrong. The auditor needs to have the same (or better) quality of reasoning as the process owner. The auditor must be able to keep the overview and not get lost in the details of the complexity.

When there are no subject matter process manuals, work descriptions, policies or procedures to be used for benchmarking the operations, the auditor needs to make up his own mind about what constitutes a best practice system of internal controls. The auditor may find such support in a work programme, but he would still need good experience in adapting the audit work to the subject matter.

This risk mitigation measure corresponds to the chapter *Performance Management*, as described in *Volume I* of *Driving Audit Value*.

ERM-4: Increase quality and standardisation of audit processes and procedures

Increase the level of quality and standardisation of the audit processes and procedures and improve the monitoring and the effectiveness of the application of these standards. Formalise and expand the audit function processes, procedures, quality assurance and improvement processes.

ERM-5: Improve supervision and quality control processes

Formalise and document the audit engagement supervision processes and procedures, and consistently apply these procedures. Work programmes and working papers must be prepared by the auditor and formally reviewed by the CAE. They must discuss the application of the testing and the results thereof to ensure that the approved audit procedures are correctly applied and the results are correctly interpreted. The CAE or audit manager should perform a thorough review of the working papers. The audit work performed should be compared with the audit plan and work programme, to identify any shortcoming in the audit execution and to rectify their impact. The more complete the working paper documentation, the lower the risk of supervising audit management overlooking topics, which the auditor might have misjudged.

For the very high profile audit engagements, the CAE should involve herself or her supervising audit managers during all the phases of the audit engagement. She must be present in all preparatory discussions of the audit objective, the audit scope, the expected results and the work programmes. Similarly, the CAE must involve herself with the review of the interim results, the weekly updates, the final results discussions, the review of the draft audit report and the closing meeting with the process owner and management.

This gives CAE, or her audit manager, the possibility to pass their own judgment on the test results. If the auditor documents an issue, but does not recognise its significance, the CAE has the possibility to confirm or reject the auditor's conclusion on the test. During the supervision process it must also be confirmed that all the work programme steps were executed as planned, or valid explanations must be provided why a step was not or only partially performed.

ERM-7: Increase internal communication and feedback
Improve the communication between the auditor and the CAE. Not only in the form of the working papers, but also through the discussions and brainstorming on the results of the audit work. The better the communication, the more the auditor can learn from the CAE, and the better the CAE can understand the results of the audit work and identify any missed issues, scope limitations, or false judgements.

ERM-8: Improve quality of working paper documentation
Have clear and strict working paper documentation rules. The working paper documentation standard must require that all tests and results thereof are documented. This documentation has four aspects: (1) the test objectives, (2) the performed audit test, (3) the test result, and (4) the conclusion of the test results against the achievement of the test objectives.

ERM-10: Increase understanding of the business, company and subject matter
Understanding the company and business, the subject matter strategies and objectives, will enable the auditors to put the audit issues in the right perspective. This should avoid overlooking significant issues, over-valuing small issues, and wrong audit conclusions. Put in substantial efforts to understand the subject matter or hire specialists in case the topics require specialised knowledge, experience and skills, not available in the audit team.

Thoroughly understanding the inherent risk and control risk profile, and the underlying process objectives and controls, will ensure that they interpret the audit test results in the perspective of management's objectives for the processes. Do not forget that a risk is defined as a potential deviation from an objective. Therefore, the CAE can only assess the potential impact of a risk when she has a good understanding of the related management objectives.

ERM-11: Improve access to critical data, information, transactions, projects, initiatives, and management
The access to critical information and the value driving aspects of the subject matter must be ensured. The better the quality and quantity of the information about the subject matter, the lower the risk of overlooking significant issues. Ensure that the access to the data, information, transactions and process staff, are sufficient for the completion of the audit testing. Such access should principally already be guaranteed prior to the start of the audit engagement.

ERM-12: Increase coordination with process owner, management and the board

Coordinate the risk mitigation with the process owner and local management to ensure its efficiency and cost-effectiveness. Improve the level of coordination (and agreement) of the audit results with the auditee, the process owner and the responsible managers. The more complex and judgmental the processes of the subject matter, the more important it is to validate the audit function's understanding of the impact of the audit issues. This ensures a correct interpretation of the risk, its impact and the required risk mitigation measures. It should avoid overlooking significant issues, over-valuing small issues, and wrong audit conclusions.

Extensively involve the auditee and process owner during the key phases of the audit. The process owner will be the expert and knows the subject matter better than anyone else. Make use of his knowledge, but maintain the audit function's independence and objectivity while developing the audit conclusions and the audit opinion. Conduct regular meetings and confirm the results and the interpretation with the process owner. Closely liaise with the other subject matter experts within the organisation.

Thoroughly discuss all the issues, significant and small, with the process owner. He will know his business better than the auditors will ever know, however, he might miss the broader perspective of the division/business unit, executive management or the board. The CAE is close to these higher levels, so she must be able to represent their perspective in the assessments.

It must be part of the process that the CAE discusses all the significant issues in a draft report with the higher management levels before formally distributing the audit report. Their perspectives will help the CAE prevent over-valuing a small issue as significant.

Risk mitigation of overlooking significant issues

ERM-3: Improve proficiency and experience of auditor/audit manager/CAE

ERM-4: Increase quality and standardisation of audit processes and procedures

ERM-5: Improve supervision and quality control processes

ERM-6: Improve focus of work programme to risk profile of subject matter

The CAE must ensure that the audit testing programme is tailor made to the risk profile of the subject matter. The focus, depth and width of the audit testing programme must encounter the risk of overlooking significant issues. The higher the complexity of the subject matter and the higher the level of ambiguity, judgement and estimates to achieve objectives within the processes of the subject matter, the more tailored the work programme should be. The quality and coverage of the work programme must be sufficient to be able to achieve the audit engagement objectives. The work programme must enforce a sufficient level of risk assessments on the objectives of the subject matter under audit.

Obtain input into the work programme from (inside or outside) auditors with the experience in reviewing the subject matter. Consider discussing the main elements of the work programme with the process owner.

Detailed supervision on the development of the work programme, using standardised work programmes for standardised situations, and using tailor made work programmes for special situations. This must ensure that the correct audit testing method is selected.

If the potential for significant risks is limited, the work programme can also be limited, only covering the basics while maintaining audit efficiency.

ERM-7: Increase internal communication and feedback
ERM-8: Improve quality of working paper documentation

ERM-9: Brainstorm on potential significant issues

In my personal experience, it was always very helpful to discuss with the audit team the potential significant issues within the subject matter prior to the start of the audit. This focuses the audit team, makes them think big, and sets the expectations of possible big issues ahead of the audit field work. It is important for the audit team to understand how the CAE thinks, and what is expected of the audit engagement. Theorise on the expected big results. Success of this risk mitigating step is rooted in the understanding of the subject matter. The CAE and her team should have a solid understanding of the topic to be audited, its inherent risk profile, as well as its control risk profile. The team has insufficient knowledge of this? Send the auditors on a pre-engagement visit for understanding the business and subject matter, before starting the field work.

When sitting together with the team to discuss the draft audit report, the CAE must revisit the brainstorming results from before the audit engagement, and discuss why these big issues were not identified or why different big issues did come up. Did it have to do with the audit work programme, the different nature of the subject matter than expected, or were the processes simply well controlled? Was the pre-audit risk assessment of the inherent risk and control risk confirmed as well? If these two risks were much higher than expected, then there must be some big issues. Did the auditors identify these?

ERM-10: Increase understanding of the business, company and subject matter

ERM-11: Improve access to critical data, information, transactions, projects, initiatives, and management

ERM-12: Increase coordination with process owner, management and the board

ERM-13: Think as management and the board

Better understand management's and the board's thinking and priorities. This enables the auditors and the CAE to think like a business manager, and to put the audit findings into the appropriate perspective. The audit team should know how executive management and the board think about the relevant topics.

ERM-14: Assess subject matter and audit results in the larger perspective

Improve the ability to assess the subject matter and the results of the testing in the larger perspective of the higher organisational units. The higher the complexity of the subject matter, the level of ambiguity, judgement and estimates to achieve the objectives within the processes of the subject matter, the more this subject matter will be an integral part of the strategies and operations of the divisions/business units, regions, group functions or the group, the more important it is to understand the broader business perspective of higher organisational management on the audit issues.

Risk mitigation of agreeing no or wrong audit issue risk mitigation measures

ERM-3: Improve proficiency and experience of auditor/audit manager/CAE

ERM-4: Increase quality and standardisation of audit processes and procedures

ERM-5: Improve supervision and quality control processes

ERM-7: Increase internal communication and feedback

ERM-8: Improve quality of working paper documentation

ERM-10: Increase understanding of the business, company and subject matter

ERM-11: Improve access to critical data, information, transactions, projects, initiatives, and management

ERM-12: Increase coordination with process owner, management and the board

ERM-13: Think as management and the board

ERM-14: Assess subject matter and audit results in the larger perspective

ERM-15: Improve appropriate risk mitigation measures for identified risks

Maintain the audit methodology that for each risk identified during the audit, an appropriate risk mitigation measure needs to be defined. This mitigation measure will depend on the level of the risk, the risk appetite and the specific nature of the risk.

Risk mitigation of wrong audit engagement conclusions

ERM-3: Improve proficiency and experience of auditor/audit manager/CAE

ERM-4: Increase quality and standardisation of audit processes and procedures

ERM-5: Improve supervision and quality control processes

ERM-6: Improve focus of work programme to risk profile of subject matter

ERM-7: Increase internal communication and feedback

ERM-8: Improve quality of working paper documentation

ERM-9: Brainstorm on potential significant issues

ERM-10: Increase understanding of the business, company and subject matter

ERM-11: Improve access to critical data, information, transactions, projects, initiatives, and management

ERM-12: Increase coordination with process owner, management and the board

ERM-13: Think as management and the board

ERM-14: Assess subject matter and audit results in the larger perspective

Risk mitigation of over-valuing small issues

ERM-3: Improve proficiency and experience of auditor/audit manager/CAE

ERM-4: Increase quality and standardisation of audit processes and procedures

ERM-5: Improve supervision and quality control processes

ERM-7: Increase internal communication and feedback

ERM-8: Improve quality of working paper documentation

ERM-9: Brainstorm on potential significant issues

ERM-10: Increase understanding of the business, company and subject matter

ERM-11: Improve access to critical data, information, transactions, projects, initiatives, and management

ERM-12: Increase coordination with process owner, management and the board

ERM-13: Think as management and the board

ERM-14: Assess subject matter and audit results in the larger perspective

Risk mitigation of overlooking scope limitations

ERM-1: Timely audit announcements and appropriate scheduling

ERM-2: Manage short-term audit capacity shortfalls

ERM-3: Improve proficiency and experience of auditor/audit manager/CAE

ERM-4: Increase quality and standardisation of audit processes and procedures

ERM-5: Improve supervision and quality control processes

ERM-6: Improve focus of work programme to risk profile of subject matter

ERM-7: Increase internal communication and feedback

ERM-8: Improve quality of working paper documentation

ERM-10: Increase understanding of the business, company and subject matter

ERM-11: Improve access to critical data, information, transactions, projects, initiatives, and management

ERM-12: Increase coordination with process owner, management and the board

ERM-13: Think as management and the board
ERM-14: Assess subject matter and audit results in the larger perspective

ERM-16: Improve process for identifying and handling scope limitations

Have a decision process and process flow for handling scope limitations. The expectations of the process owner need to be managed. In particular, the audit scope, coverage and objective need to be clearly stated. In case these deviate from what was announced at the start of the audit, the process owner needs to be informed.

The CAE must decide whether to accept the limitation, or to allocate more time to the audit to overcome the limitation. If she accepts the limitation, she must make sure that the audit report adequately reflects this, so that the right level of assurance is provided.

Audit Process Risk Mitigation

Figure 50 – Three Audit Process Risk Mitigation Categories

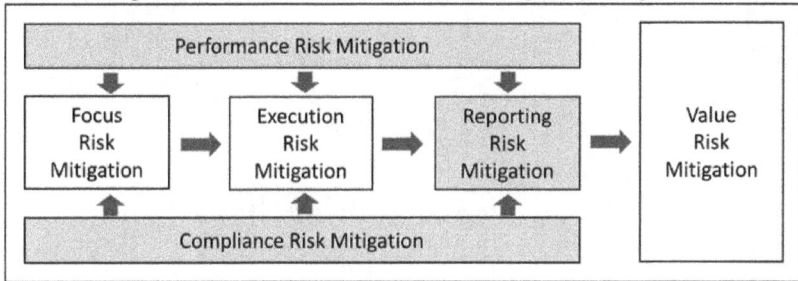

Performance Risk Mitigation			
Focus Risk Mitigation	Execution Risk Mitigation	Reporting Risk Mitigation	Value Risk Mitigation
Compliance Risk Mitigation			

In the next three chapters, each of the three audit process risk mitigation categories (performance risk mitigation, reporting risk mitigation and compliance risk mitigation), together with the 30 risk mitigation measures from the *Audit Risk Mitigation Catalogue©*, are described and analysed in detail. The chapters have the following structure:

- A risk mitigation matrix matches the risks from the *Audit Risk Mitigation Catalogue©* with the risk categories, consistent with the *Audit Process Risk Mitigation Tree©*.

- Each of the individual risk mitigation measures is described and analysed in detail. Since the majority of the individual risk mitigation measures address multiple risk subcategories, only the first subchapter for which a risk mitigation measure is applicable an elaborate explanation will be provided. In the following subchapters that repeat these mitigation measures, only the titles of these measures are listed.

Audit Process Risk Mitigation Tree©

The *Audit Process Risk Mitigation Tree©* captures all 30 mitigation measures in one chart.

Figure 51 – Audit Process Risk Mitigation Tree©

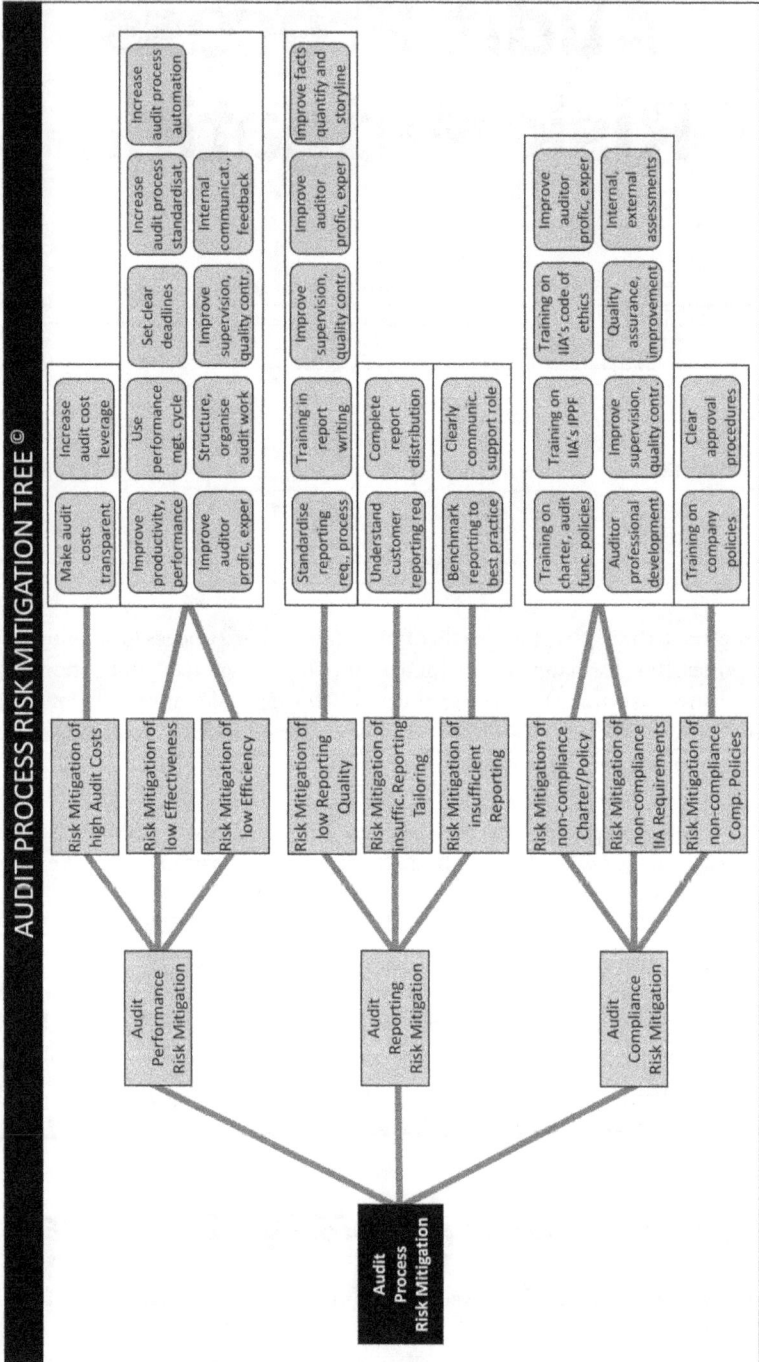

Audit Risk Mitigation 4: Performance Risk Mitigation

Figure 52 – Eleven Elements of Performance Risk Mitigation

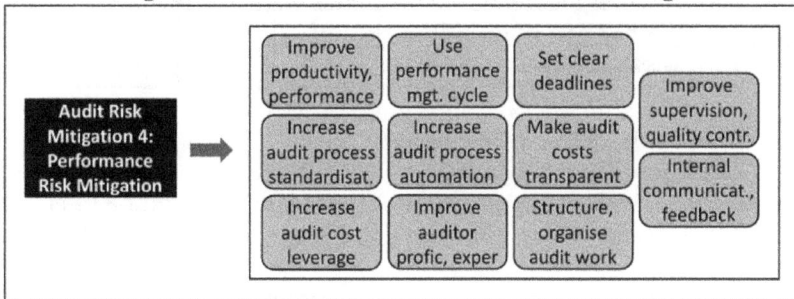

Audit Risk Mitigation 4: Performance Risk Mitigation	Improve productivity, performance	Use performance mgt. cycle	Set clear deadlines	Improve supervision, quality contr.
	Increase audit process standardisat.	Increase audit process automation	Make audit costs transparent	Internal communicat., feedback
	Increase audit cost leverage	Improve auditor profic, exper	Structure, organise audit work	

Performance risk mitigation is mitigating the risk that the audit function processes and the use of the audit resources are not effective or efficient.

In the following Performance Risk Mitigation Matrix, the 11 performance risk mitigation measures from the *Audit Risk Mitigation Catalogue©* are matched with the three performance risk categories, consistent with the *Audit Process Risk Mitigation Tree©*. The conclusions from this matrix are:

- The use of the performance management cycle is the main enabler to mitigating the performance risks relating to costs, efficiency and effectiveness.

- Nine of the 11 measures have a dual impact on efficiency as well as effectiveness.

Figure 53 – Performance Risk Mitigation Matrix

PERFORMANCE RISK MITIGATION MATRIX			
Performance Risk Mitigation: / Performance Risk Categories:	Risks of high audit costs	Risks of low effectiveness	Risks of low efficiency
PRM-1: Actively manage audit function productivity and performance	✓	✓	✓
PRM-2: Utilise performance management cycle	✓	✓	✓
PRM-3: Set clear deadlines	✓	✓	✓
PRM-4: Increase quality and standardisation of audit processes and procedures	✓	✓	✓
PRM-5: Increase automation of audit processes	✓	✓	✓
PRM-6: Make costs of audit activities transparent	✓		
PRM-7: Increase leverage of audit cost	✓		
PRM-8: Improve proficiency and experience of auditor/audit manager/CAE	✓	✓	✓
PRM-9: Better structure and organise audit work and planning		✓	✓
PRM-10: Improve supervision and quality control processes		✓	✓
PRM-11: Increase internal communication and feedback		✓	✓

The chapter is divided into three sections:
1. Risk mitigation of high audit costs (PRM-1 to 8)
2. Risk mitigation of low effectiveness (PRM-1 to 5 and PRM-8 to 11)
3. Risk mitigation of low efficiency (PRM-1 to 5 and PRM-8 to 11)

The measures required for mitigating the performance risks are elaborately described in the chapter *Performance Management* in *Volume I* of *Driving Audit Value*. For this reason, the descriptions of the mitigation measures below are kept relatively short.

Risk mitigation of high audit costs

PRM-1: Actively manage audit function productivity and performance
Actively manage the audit function's productivity and performance. Maintain a performance management methodology which enables maximisation of the output of the audit function.

PRM-2: Utilise performance management cycle
Utilise the performance management cycle and set clear goals. Set productivity targets, particularly for the audit engagements. Improve the available capacities of the auditors, to get more audit days out of an auditor.

Set performance targets that are challenging and frequently measure performance.

PRM-3: Set clear deadlines
Most people are more productive when working under pressure, so set clear deadlines for the audit engagements and the related tasks.

PRM-4: Increase quality and standardisation of audit processes and procedures
Increase the standardisation of the internal audit processes and products. This will streamline the generation of the output as it eliminates the time needed for the development of the products and processes.

PRM-5: Increase automation of audit processes
Increase the use of technology, automate as many as possible audit processes. Use electronic work flow management for audit engagement planning, working papers, supervision, working paper reviews and audit report generation.

PRM-6: Make costs of audit activities transparent
Make the costs of the audit activities transparent, for example by analysing the costs per audit engagement and audit person-day. What gets measured, gets managed. Make the audit costs transparent to enable leveraging of the audit costs.

PRM-7: Increase leverage of audit cost
Increase the level of leverage of the audit cost. Reduce the average cost per audit day to a level below the comparable costs of outsourcing. Lower the cost of the individual audit engagements by increasing the leverage, reducing the number of pages in the audit reports, streamlining and standardising the processes, shortening reviews, and using fewer auditors on an engagement. Decrease the cost of audit engagements by reducing the planned number of audit person-days according to the annual audit plan. Decrease the costs of the administrative tasks.

PRM-8: Improve proficiency and experience of auditor/audit manager/CAE
Improve the capabilities and experience of the auditor/audit manager/CAE and have qualified and experienced auditors conduct the audit. If possible, use the auditors who are familiar with the audit work and the subject matter. In the case of inexperienced auditors, increase the level of supervision. Increase the staff training and professional development. Attract and retain high-potential and qualified auditors based on qualifications such as CPA, CIA, CISA, and university degrees. Reduce the staff turnover.

Risk mitigation of low effectiveness

PRM-1: Actively manage audit function productivity and performance

PRM-2: Utilise performance management cycle

PRM-3: Set clear deadlines

PRM-4: Increase quality and standardisation of audit processes and procedures

PRM-5: Increase automation of audit processes

PRM-8: Improve proficiency and experience of auditor/audit manager/CAE

PRM-9: Better structure and organise audit work and planning

Structure and organise the audit work and planning. Provide the auditors with a clear focus on the audit engagement objectives, and set deadlines. The better organised, the quicker a task can be performed, so ensure that the people know what to do, how to do and when to do their duties. Have a structured plan (work programme) for handling a task. Standardise the processes, work programmes, audit reports, and use automated workflows. When distractions are reduced, e.g. through a clean desk policy and a good work environment, the staff will be more focused.

PRM-10: Improve supervision and quality control processes

Formalise and enhance the supervision processes. The better the supervision, the higher the chance for the CAE to positively influence the efficiency and the effectiveness of the audit processes. Though, the supervision and quality control processes also need to have an appropriate level of effectiveness and efficiency. The lower the inherent risk of the subject matter, the lower the level of supervision should be. The higher the proficiency and experience of the auditor, the lower the supervision should be.

PRM-11: Increase internal communication and feedback

Encourage open communication. The CAE should listen to the staff's concerns and address them, whether relating to their job, the company, their career, or a particular audit engagement. The CAE must give the auditors all the information they need to reach their goals and meet the expectations. In general, share the information on the developments in the business through weekly or monthly conference calls. Let them know what is going on in the company and the audit function. Specifically, for the individual audit engagements, ensure that they have all the information they need to reach their engagement objectives. Provide the team members with regular feedback on their performance, and they will do better. Give immediate feedback when an auditor can improve something. Do not wait until the end of the year and go through a long list then. The sooner they know, the sooner they can improve their performance. Give positive feedback each day and give recognition to what they do well.

Risk mitigation of low efficiency

PRM-1:   Actively manage audit function productivity and performance
PRM-2:   Utilise performance management cycle
PRM-3:   Set clear deadlines
PRM-4:   Increase quality and standardisation of audit processes and procedures
PRM-5:   Increase automation of audit processes
PRM-8:   Improve proficiency and experience of auditor/audit manager/CAE
PRM-9:   Better structure and organise audit work and planning
PRM-10: Improve supervision and quality control processes
PRM-11: Increase internal communication and feedback

Audit Risk Mitigation 5: Reporting Risk Mitigation

Figure 54 – Nine Elements of Reporting Risk Mitigation

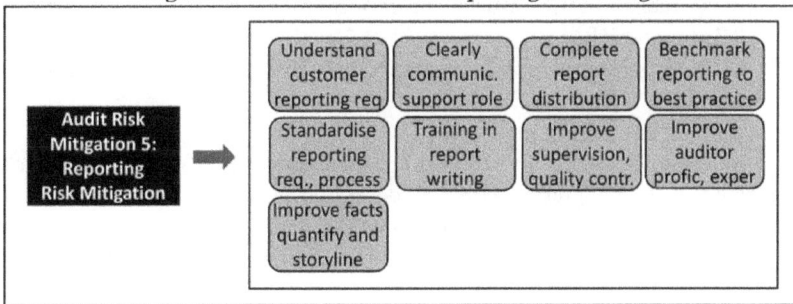

Audit Risk Mitigation 5: Reporting Risk Mitigation	⟹	Understand customer reporting req	Clearly communic. support role	Complete report distribution	Benchmark reporting to best practice
		Standardise reporting req., process	Training in report writing	Improve supervision, quality contr.	Improve auditor profic, exper
		Improve facts quantify and storyline			

Reporting risk mitigation is mitigating the risk that the audit reporting does not accurately and completely reflect the audit function's activities and the achievement of the customer value proposition.

In the following Reporting Risk Mitigation Matrix, the nine reporting risk mitigation measures from the *Audit Risk Mitigation Catalogue*© are matched with the three reporting risk categories, consistent with the *Audit Process Risk Mitigation Tree*©. The conclusions from this matrix are:

- The auditor's proficiency in writing audit reports and the supervision over the reporting processes are the biggest levers for mitigating the reporting risks.

- Understanding the customer's requirements contributes to adding value, while the standardisation of the reporting processes enhances the efficiency and effectiveness.

Figure 55 – Reporting Risk Mitigation Matrix

REPORTING RISK MITIGATION MATRIX	Risks of low reporting quality	Risks of insufficient reporting tailoring	Risks of insufficient reporting
Reporting Risk Categories: / *Reporting Risk Mitigations:*			
RRM-1: Increase understanding of reporting requirements from key customers	✓	✓	✓
RRM-2: Clear communications about differences between assurance and support/consulting			✓
RRM-3: Critically review completeness of audit report distribution list		✓	
RRM-4: Benchmark audit function reporting against best practices	✓		✓
RRM-5: Increase standardisation of reporting requirements and processes	✓		
PRM-6: Improve proficiency and experience of auditor/audit manager/CAE	✓	✓	✓
RRM-7: Train auditors in writing business-like audit reports	✓		
RRM-8: Improve supervision and quality control processes	✓	✓	✓
RRM-9: Improve facts, quantifications and storyline	✓		

The chapter is divided into three sections:
1. Risk mitigation of low reporting quality (RRM-1, RRM-4 to 9)
2. Risk mitigation of insufficient reporting tailoring (RRM-1, RRM-3, RRM-6 and RRM-8)
3. Risk mitigation of insufficient reporting (RRM-1 and 2, RRM-4, RRM-6 and RRM-8)

The measures required for mitigating the reporting risks are elaborately described in the chapter *Reporting*, as described in *Volume I* of *Driving Audit Value*. For this reason, the descriptions of the mitigation measures below are kept relatively short.

Risk mitigation of low reporting quality

RRM-1: Increase understanding of reporting requirements from key customers
Increasing the level of understanding of the reporting requirements from the key customers. Know what the board and executive management expect of the audit reporting, and adjust the reporting to accommodate their requirements. Also think about the structured and consistent verbal reporting.

RRM-4: Benchmark audit function reporting against best practices
Benchmarking the audit reporting against the best practices and increase the creativity in capturing the main elements of the performance of the audit function for the benefit of communicating the added-value contribution. Think about the knowledge sharing and the annual report of the audit

function. The CAE should be creative in the ways that the achievement of the customer value proposition can be reported.

RRM-5: Increase standardisation of reporting requirements and processes

Increasing the level of standardisation and the clarity of the reporting requirements and processes. Set clear performance standards and define and standardise the audit reports, distribution lists, writing styles, format, style, layout, and so forth. Make sure that the audit reports have clear wording and messages. Reduce the number of pages of the reports to the minimum.

RRM-6: Improve proficiency and experience of auditor/audit manager/CAE

The better the proficiency and experience of the auditor/audit manager/CAE, the better the quality of the audit reports will be.

RRM-7: Train auditors in writing business-like audit reports

Improve the auditors' proficiency in writing business-like audit reports. Provide training on the job as well as in special report writing courses.

RRM-8: Improve supervision and quality control processes

Increasing the level of supervision over the audit reports written by those auditors of whom the CAE knows that they have weak writing skills. The CAE should have elaborate discussions with the auditors about understanding and formulating the critical elements (such as the conclusions, opinions, ratings, risk impacts, and other judgemental areas) in the audit reports.

RRM-9: Improve facts, quantifications and storyline

Ensure that all the reports present sufficient facts and quantifications of the topics, issues and risks. Eliminate the subjectivity and bias, and reduce the judgement from the reporting.

Risk mitigation of insufficient reporting tailoring

RRM-1: Increase understanding of reporting requirements from key customers

RRM-3: Critically review completeness of audit report distribution list

Understand who needs to benefit from the audit reporting and ensure that all those relevant are included on the distribution list. This includes auditees, process owners, local management, division/business unit management, regional management, brand management, functional management, executive management, management of the 2nd line of defence, and the board.

RRM-6: Improve proficiency and experience of auditor/audit manager/CAE

RRM-8: Improve supervision and quality control processes

Risk mitigation of insufficient reporting

RRM-1: Increase understanding of reporting requirements from key customers

RRM-2: Clear communications about differences between assurance and support/consulting

The CAE must be clear in the communications about the differences between audit assurance and support/consulting work. In the audit and consulting announcements, ensure that the relevant people are included on the distribution list and clearly state the objectives of the activities, to avoid confusion with respect to the level of assurance.

RRM-4: Benchmark audit function reporting against best practices

RRM-6: Improve proficiency and experience of auditor/audit manager/CAE

RRM-8: Improve supervision and quality control processes

Audit Risk Mitigation 6: Compliance Risk Mitigation

Figure 56 – Ten Elements of Compliance Risk Mitigation

Audit Risk Mitigation 6: Compliance Risk Mitigation	Training on charter, audit func. policies	Training on IIA's IPPF	Training on IIA's code of ethics	Improve auditor profic, exper
	Auditor professional development	Improve supervision, quality contr.	Quality assurance, improvement	Internal, external assessments
	Training on company policies	Clear approval procedures		

Compliance risk mitigation is mitigating the risk that the audit activities conducted by the department and auditors are not compliant with the internal and external laws, regulations and policies.

In the following Compliance Risk Mitigation Matrix, the 10 compliance risk mitigation measures from the *Audit Risk Mitigation Catalogue©* are matched with the three compliance risk categories, consistent with the *Audit Process Risk Mitigation Tree©*. The conclusions from this matrix are:

- The most effective method for mitigating the compliance risk is having comprehensive audit function policies and procedures, and training the auditors in these requirements.

- The risk mitigation of poor audit practices is mostly driven by applying the requirements from The IIA's IPPF and maintaining an effective quality assurance and improvement programme.

Figure 57 – Compliance Risk Mitigation Matrix

COMPLIANCE RISK MITIGATION MATRIX			
Compliance Risks Categories: Compliance Risk Mitigations:	Risks of non-compliance with audit charter and policies	Risks of non-compliance with IIA requirements	Risks of non-compliance with company policies
CRM-1: Train audit team on content of audit charter and audit function policies	✓	✓	
CRM-2: Improve proficiency and experience of auditor/audit manager/CAE	✓	✓	
CRM-3: Set up professional development programme for each auditor	✓	✓	
CRM-4: Train auditors on IIA's IPPF requirements	✓	✓	
CRM-5: Discuss and sign code of ethics	✓	✓	
CRM-6: Improve supervision and quality control processes	✓	✓	✓
CRM-7: Maintain effective quality assurance and improvement programme	✓	✓	
CRM-8: Regularly perform internal quality self-assessments and periodically engage external assessor	✓	✓	
CRM-9: Training on company policies and administrative procedures	✓		✓
CRM-10: Clear approval procedures	✓	✓	✓

The chapter is divided into three sections:
1 Risk mitigation of non-compliance with the audit charter and the audit function policies (CRM-1 to 10)
2. Risk mitigation of non-compliance with The IIA's professional requirements (CRM-1 to 8 and CRM-10)
3. Risk mitigation of non-compliance with the company policies (CRM-6, CRM-9 and CRM-10)

Risk mitigation of non-compliance with audit charter and policies

CRM-1: Train audit team on content of audit charter and audit function policies

Train the audit team on the content of the audit charter and the audit function policies. New auditors should be trained during the onboarding process and receive a closer supervision.

CRM-2: Improve proficiency and experience of auditor/audit manager/CAE

Improve the proficiency and experience of the auditor/audit manager/CAE.

CRM-3: Set up professional development programme for each auditor
Set up a personal development programme for each auditor to enhance the audit practices and professional growth.

CRM-4: Train auditors on IIA's IPPF requirements
Train the auditors on The IIA's IPPF requirements, for example through the CIA professional certification.

CRM-5: Discuss and sign code of ethics
Each year, the audit team should discuss and sign the code of ethics. Discuss the potential and resolutions for conflict of interest, unethical behaviour, and subjectivity and bias in the activities of the audit function.

CRM-6: Improve supervision and quality control processes
Formalise the supervision and quality control processes and ensure that they are effectively applied.

CRM-7: Maintain effective quality assurance and improvement programme
Maintain a quality assurance and improvement programme, to ensure that the audit function delivers added value through structured and focused internal processes. The CAE should frequently assess the status and closely monitor the improvements.

CRM-8: Regularly perform internal quality self-assessments and periodically engage external assessor
Perform frequent self-assessments until satisfied with the quality, and periodically have an external assessment done, consistent with the requirements from the IIA.

CRM-9: Training on company policies and administrative procedures
Train the audit team on the relevant company policies and administrative procedures, such as expense reporting, performance evaluations, budgeting, and so forth. New auditors should be trained during the onboarding process and receive a closer supervision. The CAE must have a good understanding of the corporate policies and ensure that these are reflected in the audit handbook.

CRM-10: Clear approval procedures
Enhance the quality of the approval procedures for the administrative processes in the audit function.

Risk mitigation of non-compliance with IIA requirements

CRM-1: Train audit team on content of audit charter and audit function policies

CRM-2: Improve proficiency and experience of auditor/audit manager/CAE

CRM-3: Set up professional development programme for each auditor

CRM-4: Train auditors on IIA's IPPF requirements

CRM-5: Discuss and sign code of ethics

CRM-6: Improve supervision and quality control processes

CRM-7: Maintain effective quality assurance and improvement

CRM-8: Regularly perform internal quality self-assessments and periodically engage external assessor

CRM-10: Clear approval procedures

Risk mitigation of non-compliance with company policies

CRM-6: Improve supervision and quality control processes

CRM-9: Training on company policies and administrative procedures

CRM-10: Clear approval procedures

Impact of Company Inherent and Control Risk

This last chapter provides a brief view on the impact of the company's and subject matter's inherent risks and control risks. This is the part of the *Beumer Audit Risk Management Model©* in the top-left quadrant (with the light-grey colour background), which is not discussed in this book, as it relates to management's risk management processes (as opposed to the audit function's risk management processes). Still the inherent and control risks contained in the company's risk universe (which includes the subject matter's inherent and control risks) have an impact on the level of the audit risk mitigation.

The CAE needs to keep the audit assurance risk at the level of the risk appetite of the board. Once the CAE understands the risk profile of the subject matter, he needs to manage his assurance risk within the audit engagement processes to compensate for the subject matter's inherent and control risks. A low assurance risk means that the audit engagement processes and procedures must be so good that the audit work captures all the subject matter's risks of significant deviations from achieving their strategies and objectives.

In case of high inherent and control risks, the CAE cannot rely on the subject matter's control and risk management processes to capture and manage the business risks. He needs to maintain a high level of audit risk mitigation in his procedures and processes.

Conversely, low inherent and control risks mean that he can rely on management's control and risk management processes to timely identify and appropriately manage risks to the achievement of the company's strategies and objectives. In this case he can maintain a standard level of audit risk mitigation in his audit procedures and processes.

The same is valid at the audit function level, particularly for the development of the annual audit plan and the CAE's overarching controls over the execution of the annual audit plan.

The two following figures provide a high-level summary of the impact of the level of the inherent risk and control risk, of the company and the subject matter, on the nature and level of the audit risk mitigation measures. These figures capture the audit assurance risk mitigation in a simplified way.

Volume III of *Driving Audit Value: Audit Engagement Strategy* gives more details about the subject matter inherent and control risk assessments.

Figure 58 – Impact of Subject Matter Risk Profile

Impact of Subject Matter Risk Profile on Audit Assurance Risk Mitigation				
	Subject Matter Inherent Risk is		Subject Matter Control Risk is		CAE's Risk Mitigating Actions to achieve an acceptable level of Audit Assurance Risk should be
IF	High	AND	High	THEN	• High understanding of subject matter • High level of coordination during the audit engagement planning and execution • High proficiency and quality of the auditors • High number of substantive/process tests • High focused and detailed work programmes • High quality supervision processes
	High		Low		• High understanding of subject matter • High level of coordination during the audit engagement planning and execution • High proficiency and quality of the auditors • Standard number of substantive/process tests • Standard focused and detailed work programmes • Standard quality supervision processes
	Low		High		• Standard understanding of subject matter • Standard level of coordination during the audit engagement planning and execution • Standard proficiency and quality of the auditors • High number of substantive/process tests • High focused and detailed work programmes • High quality supervision processes
	Low		Low		• Standard understanding of subject matter • Standard level of coordination during the audit engagement planning and execution • Standard proficiency and quality of the auditors • Standard number of substantive/process tests • Standard focused and detailed work programmes • Standard quality supervision processes

Figure 59 – Impact of Company Risk Profile

Impact of Company Risk Profile on Audit Assurance Risk Mitigation				
Company Inherent Risk is		Company Control Risk is		CAE's Risk Mitigating Actions to achieve an acceptable level of Audit Assurance Risk should be
High		High		• High understanding of business and strategies • High level of coordination in annual audit planning • High proficiency and quality audit managers • High focus (duration, depth, frequency) in audits • High formalised IA function processes, procedures • High quality assurance, improvement programme
High		Low		• High understanding of business and strategies • High level of coordination in annual audit planning • High proficiency and quality audit managers • Standard focus (duration, depth, frequency) in audits • Standard formalised IA function processes, procedures • Standard quality assurance, improvement programme
Low		High		• Standard understanding of business and strategies • Standard level of coordination in annual audit planning • Standard proficiency and quality audit managers • High focus (duration, depth, frequency) in audits • High formalised IA function processes, procedures • High quality assurance, improvement programme
Low		Low		• Standard understanding of business and strategies • Standard level of coordination in annual audit planning • Standard proficiency and quality audit managers • Standard focus (duration, depth, frequency) in audits • Standard formalised IA function processes, procedures • Standard quality assurance, improvement programme

(IF ... AND ... THEN)

VOL. I OF DRIVING AUDIT VALUE:

AUDIT FUNCTION STRATEGY

Volume I of *Driving Audit Value: Audit function Strategy*. This *Volume I* describes the strategies for creating the maximum audit added value at the level of the audit function. The book explains and analyses the two main value drivers and the six main value enablers. The first edition was published in January 2017, and is available as:

-Hardcover: ISBN 978-3-906861-13-5
-EBook: ISBN 978-3-906861-14-2

Figure 60 – The Structure of Volume I of
Driving Audit Value: Audit Function Strategy

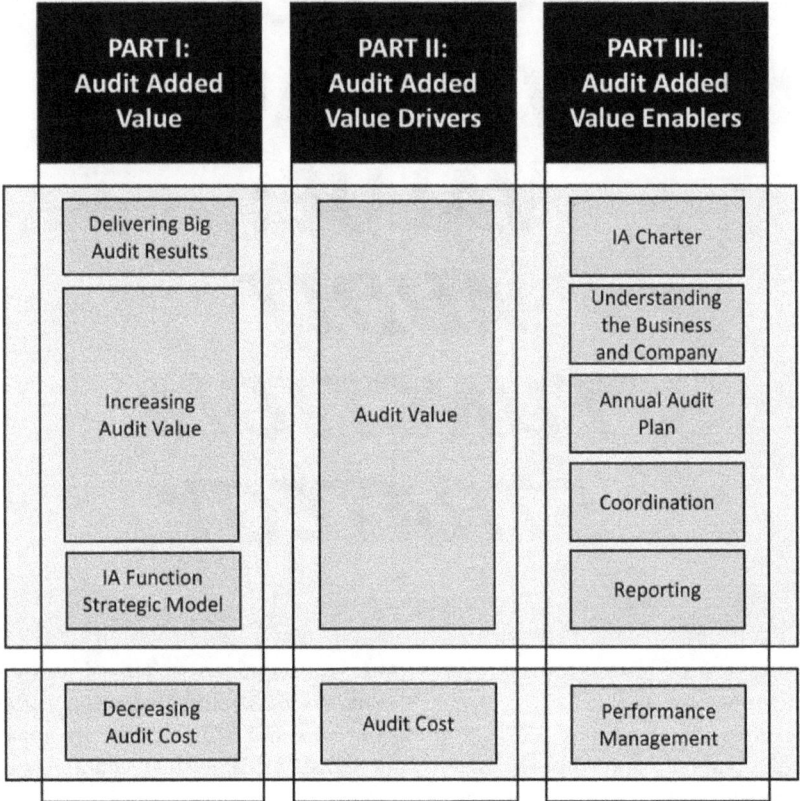

PART I: Audit Added Value	PART II: Audit Added Value Drivers	PART III: Audit Added Value Enablers
Delivering Big Audit Results		IA Charter
		Understanding the Business and Company
Increasing Audit Value	Audit Value	Annual Audit Plan
		Coordination
IA Function Strategic Model		Reporting
Decreasing Audit Cost	Audit Cost	Performance Management

Global Recognition for

AUDIT FUNCTION STRATEGY
DRIVING AUDIT VALUE (VOL. I)

"Audit Function Strategy offers profound insights and hands-on advice on the achievement of the highest performance levels for Internal Audit. The book will prove to be a bible for all Chief Audit Executives who strive to deliver the best audit value to the organisation they serve. Driving Audit Value (Vol. I) also guides Audit Committees and Executive Management for what can be expected of a state-of-the-art Internal Audit function and how to benefit from unlocked audit potentials."

Henk van Blokland, Head of Internal Audit
OC Oerlikon Management AG, Switzerland

"Hans Beumer has developed an excellent internal audit resource with thought-provoking strategies and concepts based on actual experience. Relevant and practical for new or experienced practitioners. Truly passionate about the value of internal audit to organizations."

Robert Kuling, Chairman of the Board of
Directors for IIA North America,
Partner - Risk Advisory, Deloitte, Canada

"The question 'how can internal audit truly add value' is probably as old as the profession itself. The book of Hans Beumer provides – for the first time – a holistic, in-depth analysis of how audit value is created (or destroyed) and what strategies the CAE has to optimize it. Like a forensic surgeon, Beumer decomposes the elements and drivers of audit value and provides practical context and guidance from his rich practical experience as CAE and internal audit practitioner."

Markus T. Schweizer, Managing Partner,
Strategic Solutions, Germany / Switzerland /
Austria, Ernst & Young Ltd., Switzerland

"The author describes "*Audit Function Strategy*" by cracking the value code of internal auditing in an amazing way, that can be considered as a real blueprint and "must have" for all ambitious internal auditors and CAEs. Especially the hints regarding an overarching internal audit strategy and the different value trees were a big pleasure to read. In summary, this book offers an outstanding blend of guidance, best practice and real life examples that help to improve."

Torben Hilbertz, SVP Internal Audit
Abu Dhabi Airports, Abu Dhabi, UAE

"*Audit Function Strategy* provides a crystal clear and easy to follow road map for enhancing the strategic value of the internal audit activity. This book tells you both how to maximise the added value and evaluate your progression. Hans Beumer takes the internal audit theory and best practice and makes it applicable, sharp, measurable and actionable. This book will have a profound impact on the improvement of internal audit activities in companies worldwide, as it closely ties the internal audit's customer value proposition to the expectations of companies' boards, management and other key stakeholders."

Kurt Hausheer, retired Chairman of the Audit Committee and Board of Directors member of OC Oerlikon from 2008 to 2015, and former Managing Partner Advisory at PwC, Switzerland

"The Author has done a flawless job in writing this monumental book for the internal audit professionals. Each section of this book is carefully backed with detailed illustrations, and it goes a long way towards promoting a state of the art internal audit function. This book will be a good investment and will be a collector's items for the internal audit professionals."

Jareen Yao, Director – Internal Audit, Risk & Compliance, KPMG Services Pte. Ltd. Singapore

VOL. III OF DRIVING AUDIT VALUE:

AUDIT ENGAGEMENT STRATEGY

Volume III of *Driving Audit Value: Audit Engagement Strategy*. The strategic model for driving the audit value at the level of the audit engagements is described in *Volume III*. At the audit engagement level the audit added value, value drivers, and value enablers also exist, though with a different content when compared to the level of the audit function. The first edition will be available from July 2017 as:

-Hardcover: ISBN 978-3-906861-17-3
-EBook: ISBN 978-3-906861-18-0

Figure 61 – The Structure of Volume III of Driving Audit Value:
Audit Engagement Strategy

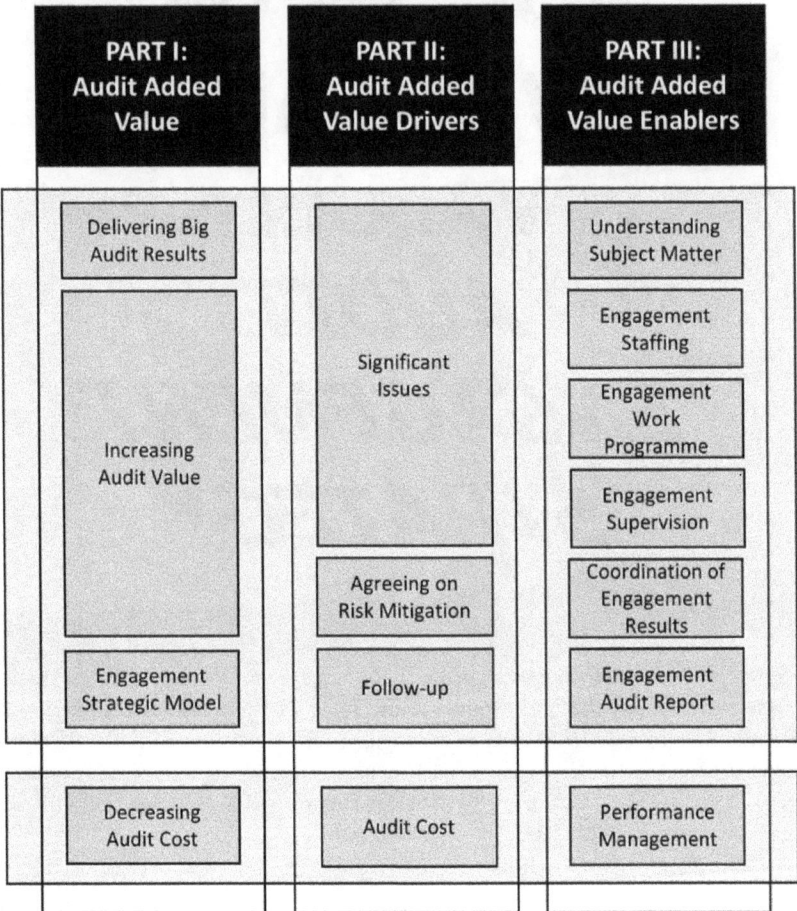

PART I: Audit Added Value	PART II: Audit Added Value Drivers	PART III: Audit Added Value Enablers
Delivering Big Audit Results		Understanding Subject Matter
Increasing Audit Value	Significant Issues	Engagement Staffing
		Engagement Work Programme
		Engagement Supervision
	Agreeing on Risk Mitigation	Coordination of Engagement Results
Engagement Strategic Model	Follow-up	Engagement Audit Report
Decreasing Audit Cost	Audit Cost	Performance Management

ABOUT THE AUTHOR

drs. Hans Beumer has a Master degree in Business Economics and was educated and trained as a Dutch CPA (Certified Public Accountant), CIA (Certified Internal Auditor), CISA (Certified Information Systems Auditor), CRMA (Certified Risk Management Auditor) and CFE (Certified Fraud Examiner).

Hans is a long-time Audit, Internal Audit and Finance Management professional. He worked for 16 years as CAE, 6 years in public accounting, and was CFO, Head of Corporate Finance, and Head Group Accounting and Reporting as well. After switching from public accounting to industry, he always worked at head offices of global operating companies.

During the last ten years, he published eight articles on the topic of internal audit in professional IA magazines in Switzerland and the USA. In 2013 he was interviewed by the leading Swiss National newspaper *NZZ*, which published an article about his innovative views on internal audit.

Since 2016 Hans is a full-time author.

Contact information: www.hansbeumer.com

www.ingramcontent.com/pod-product-compliance
Lightning Source LLC
Chambersburg PA
CBHW020210290326
41948CB00022B/264/J